PRAISE

'Discovering and then chasing our dreams is what drives us forward, bringing passion and purpose to our lives. Finally we have a book that will unlock your dreams and help you start achieving them.'
- ALISA CAMPLIN-WARNER -
WINNER OF A REMARKABLE OLYMPIC GOLD MEDAL

'Kristina's book provides the key to tap the dreams in our heart, gives us permission to claim our greatest purpose, and provides us with the tools to forge a brighter path – for all. Kristina tenderly and fiercely speaks to our hearts – to find strength and awaken our dreams to connect to something greater than ourselves.'
- DR TERERAI TRENT -
OPRAH WINFREY'S ALL-TIME FAVOURITE GUEST

'I know well the power of dreaming and of writing those dreams down on paper. It's truly life transforming. Kristina's book not only gives you permission, it shows you how, in a simple and practical no-nonsense way.'
- LI CUNXIN -
BESTSELLING AUTHOR OF *MAO'S LAST DANCER*

'The insights on dreaming and doing in this beautiful book open you to a flow of ideas and inspiration from your brain and your heart – and you never know where the learnings on offer might lead you! Awakening to your dreams and the immense possibilities they foster serves not only your quality of and excitement for life but that of the world.'
- DR LIBBY WEAVER -
LEADING NUTRITIONAL BIOCHEMIST, AN ELEVEN-TIME BESTSELLING AUTHOR AND INTERNATIONAL SPEAKER

ABOUT KRISTINA

Kristina Karlsson is the founder and Creative Director of global Swedish design and stationery business, kikki.K (102 kikki.K stores, stocked in another 250 and sold online to stationery and design lovers in more than 147 countries worldwide). She's also a sought-after international speaker, a passionate learner and self-improver – and the proud mother of two children, Axel and Tiffany, with her partner, Paul.

After growing up on a small farm in country Sweden, at the age of twenty-two she found herself in a new country, half a world away from family and friends, with little money and no idea what to do with her life. So what was a girl to do? Imagine what her dream life could look like – and then make it happen.

With deep personal experience of the power of dreaming and then doing, Kristina is on a mission to encourage people the world over to follow their own dreams.

Her new dream is to inspire and empower 101 million people just like you to write their own dreams on paper and set about bringing them to life.

Why? Because by dreaming, we can all help make the world a better place, starting with us.

KRISTINA KARLSSON

YOUR DREAM LIFE STARTS HERE

ESSENTIAL AND SIMPLE STEPS TO CREATING
THE LIFE OF YOUR DREAMS

DREAMS DON'T WORK

UNLESS YOU DO.

– JOHN C. MAXWELL –

DEDICATION

THIS BOOK IS DEDICATED TO YOU, OUR CHILDREN, MY KIKKI.K FAMILY,
AND TO THE 101 MILLION FUTURE DREAMERS OF THE WORLD, WHOSE
IMAGININGS AND REIMAGININGS WILL SHAPE THEIR LIVES, THE LIVES OF THEIR
LOVED ONES AND THE WORLD FOR GENERATIONS TO COME.

THANKS
A VERY BIG THANK YOU TO MY LIFE PARTNER AND CO-CREATOR
IN SO MANY WAYS, PAUL. YOU ARE TRULY THE WIND BENEATH MY WINGS AND AS
ALWAYS YOUR CONTRIBUTION IS INSEPARABLE FROM MINE. I LOVE OUR DREAMS.

A MASSIVE THANK YOU TO THE INSPIRING HEROES OF MINE WHO HAVE LENT
THEIR SUPPORT AND ALLOWED ME TO SHARE THEIR STORIES WITH YOU IN
THE PAGES AHEAD – SO THAT TOGETHER WE CAN INSPIRE AND EMPOWER
101 MILLION PEOPLE THE WORLD OVER TO DREAM AND DO. IN ORDER OF
APPEARANCE IN THE BOOK, HEARTFELT THANKS TO DR TERERAI TRENT,
ARIANNA HUFFINGTON, LI CUNXIN, LISA LEMKE, STELLA MCCARTNEY,
YVONNE HALLGREN, OPRAH WINFREY, SIR RICHARD BRANSON
AND ALISA CAMPLIN-WARNER.

AND TO MICHELLE OBAMA WHO I ADMIRE ENORMOUSLY. THANK YOU
FOR ALL YOU HAVE DONE AND ALL THAT YOU DO FOR MILLIONS BY
JUST BEING YOURSELF. I HOPE YOU KNOW HOW YOUR WORDS – WHICH
I'VE SOURCED FROM PUBLIC SOURCES – WILL LIFT PEOPLE UP.

COLLECTIVELY YOUR STORIES WILL SPARK DREAMS THAT WILL CREATE WAVES
OF POSITIVITY AROUND THE WORLD.

AND TO TERERAI … I AM INCREDIBLY EXCITED TO BE DONATING US$1 FROM THE
SALE OF EVERY BOOK TO THE TERERAI TRENT INTERNATIONAL FOUNDATION,
TO HELP YOU BUILD ON THE GENEROUS FOUNDATIONAL SUPPORT YOU RECEIVED
FROM OPRAH WINFREY, AND TO HELP ELEVATE YOUR DREAMS OF BRINGING
UNIVERSAL ACCESS TO QUALITY EDUCATION FOR CHILDREN, REGARDLESS OF
THEIR GENDER OR SOCIO-ECONOMIC BACKGROUNDS. FOR YOU TERERAI,
I HOPE WE SELL A MILLION BOOKS!

CONTENTS

UNDERSTAND THAT THE RIGHT

TO CHOOSE YOUR OWN PATH

IS A SACRED PRIVILEGE. USE IT.

DWELL IN POSSIBILITY.

- OPRAH WINFREY -

INSPIRING STORIES
AND WISDOM

FROM MY HEART TO YOURS

'YOUR IMAGINATION IS YOUR PREVIEW
OF LIFE'S COMING ATTRACTIONS.'

– ATTRIBUTED TO ALBERT EINSTEIN –

Imagine this. At the age of twenty-two, sleepless at 3am one morning, I woke my partner, Paul. 'What am I going to do with my life?' I whispered more than once in frustration. I'd been restless for months, having just moved to a new country, and still getting to grips with a new culture, a new language, a new life. I missed my native Sweden desperately, my family and friends. I'd had some great life experiences, but no university education, and much of my work experience till then had been in hospitality – mostly as a waitress.

I was living pay cheque to pay cheque. I felt frustrated. I felt stuck. I had no idea what I was going to do with my life, and I craved direction and purpose.

'Grab a pen and a notepad,' he said groggily, but surprisingly patiently for that hour in the morning. 'Let's write down on paper what's important to you. Let's see if we can help you get some direction.'

What ended up on paper that night was what I now call my 3am List. I certainly didn't know it at the time, but that night Paul inspired and empowered me to really dream. It was to be a profoundly pivotal moment in my life.

Neither of us realised exactly what we were doing or where it would take us, but in that 3am moment of personal angst, Paul challenged me to cast aside all constraints, all limiting thoughts, all complaints and frustrations, all of my head-driven thinking. He dared me to connect with my heart and my feelings, and to dream about what I really wanted from life at that point in time.

My 3am List was the first time in my life I'd put my dreams on paper and the power of this one simple act was remarkable. It gave me a crystal-clear sense of how my dream life could be, and the feeling was exhilarating.

On my 3am List was the following:

+ *A career I'll love driving to work for every Monday morning – doing something I'm passionate about, which gives me a sense of meaning and which I'll love!*

+ *Something that will keep me in touch with my family and friends in Sweden (I loved my new country, having moved to Melbourne from my native Sweden, but had been feeling really homesick and wanted to find a long-term solution that drew together the best of both worlds)*

+ *Something that can be a business of my own (I loved the idea of the freedom it might provide and the life I could build around that – little did I know how much hard work and how long that would take)*

+ *Earn $500 a week (the amount I felt I needed to live on and to be able to call home regularly – phone calls were very expensive in those days!)*

That simple list of my dreams, written on paper, was the catalyst for me setting out in my early twenties – with almost no money, no training, no experience, English as a second language … but with bucketloads of passion, drive and a couple of well-stretched credit cards – to start up what would become a globally loved brand and to build my dream life.

I know that we can all make dreams come true.

I've experienced firsthand the power of dreaming and know it's something anyone can do anytime, anywhere. It's free and the process can be learnt – and it really is a process, or a practice. The more you do it, the better you become.

Something magical happens when you dream, and something even more powerful happens when you write your dreams down on paper. It brings the intangible within reach, the unclear into the spotlight ... it's a life-changing process.

But few of us enter adulthood embracing the power of dreaming. Even fewer venture past merely wishing and hoping into purposefully pursuing our dreams. Instead, many of us drift or race through our days, settling for the ordinary or just trying to survive, when we could be seizing the opportunity of each precious new day to create and live our dream lives.

This is what I want to change.

For as long as I can remember, I've had a restless desire to live an amazing life – to travel the world, meet inspiring people, experience wonderful things, learn and do something meaningful with this one life I've been given. These big dreams were a world away from my upbringing on a little farm in country Sweden but, after a wildly thrilling ride, I now find myself living what to me is my dream life.

I have to pinch myself sometimes when I think about the way these dreams of mine have come true – and now I want to share what I've learnt with you.

So ... what does it mean to live your dream life?

Let's get one thing straight; it isn't about aiming for a fairytale or a perfect fantasy. Life doesn't have to be perfect to be wonderful. It throws so many ups and downs and surprises, and our lives will always be influenced by events outside our control.

YOUR DREAM LIFE

YOUR DREAM LIFE – WHATEVER THAT MEANS FOR YOU – IS A
LIFE YOU LOVE, CONSCIOUSLY DESIGNED BY YOU, FOR YOU.

A DREAM LIFE IS NOT ABOUT CREATING A FANTASY OR
LIVING SOMEONE ELSE'S LIFE OR HAVING A 'PERFECT' LIFE,
WHATEVER THAT MIGHT MEAN. IT'S ABOUT BECOMING
SOMETHING MORE, NOT SOMETHING ELSE. IT'S ABOUT
PROGRESS, NOT PERFECTION.

MOST IMPORTANTLY, IT'S ABOUT CONNECTING WITH YOUR
UNIQUE POTENTIAL, TAKING TIME OUT TO IMAGINE HOW YOU
WANT YOUR FUTURE TO BE FOR YOU AND YOUR LOVED ONES,
AND THEN CREATING IT.

When I stopped some time ago to reflect on how my dreams have become a reality, it was clear to me that I'm just one of hundreds of millions of people who have imagined what they want for their life – big and small – and then set about making it happen.

Every human achievement begins as someone's dream.

Think of the Wright brothers who imagined what it might be like to fly. Einstein, Mandela and Martin Luther King Jr whose dreams had such a big influence on the world. And people in war-ravaged countries whose desperate hopes and dreams for survival, peace and freedom drive them to extraordinary lengths to transform their lives and the lives of their loved ones.

Learning how to improve my life is something I'm totally passionate about. I absolutely LOVE hearing about what other people do to move towards living their dream lives – whatever that means for them. I love hearing the little details: their routines, practices and habits; how they take notes; how they move forward; what inspires them; what scares them; what keeps them awake at night ... what they've learnt from their biggest mistakes.

In this book you'll read the inspiring stories and wisdom of people like Dr Tererai Trent (Oprah Winfrey's all-time favourite guest), Arianna Huffington, Stella McCartney, Sir Richard Branson, Oprah Winfrey, Li Cunxin (*Mao's Last Dancer*), Alisa Camplin-Warner and others – stories that will show you how to harness the power of dreaming to genuinely transform your life.

I've spent years collecting inspiration from others, trying things out for myself and then building the things that make sense (to me) into my life. Which brings me to my reason for writing this book ... I literally get asked this one question thousands of times a year when I speak at conferences and events: 'I want to live a great life, but where do I start?'

This book is my answer.

I want to share what I've learnt and inspire people – to shed light on the simple process of dreaming, to help people ignite their creativity and imagine the future they want for themselves and their loved ones, and then set about making it happen.

Why?

I want to do my bit to make the world a better place for my children and their children – for everyone's children. With so much fundamental change happening all around us and so much uncertainty in the world, it's an important time to think about how we can all pursue our dreams and in doing so contribute to making the world a better place for all.

I'm so proud that in the last year alone via kikki.K we've shared inspiration on the power of dreaming with millions of people around the world via our products, workshops, physical and online stores, and social channels – and we're really only just getting started.

INTRODUCTION

If I was able to find a way to transform my own life so profoundly from very humble beginnings, by following a very simple process of dreaming and then doing, then you can do the same.

My theory is that the only reason people don't consistently practise dreaming in their lives is because they haven't been taught how. I want to change that by sharing the message far and wide, and inspiring the world to dream.

My promise to you is that your dream life truly does start here – *if you want it to and if you take responsibility for making it happen.*

If you have ever wanted something more from life, something different, but not known where to begin, this book is for you. It's filled with powerful ideas and simple proven tools that will help you transform those wishes into dreams and into an achievable one-page dream roadmap for creating your dream life – a life designed by you for you, and for your loved ones.

What happens next is up to you. My experience is that none of us ever dream big enough. Even though your dreams may look big and seemingly impossible when you first write them down, one day I know you'll look back and realise you could have dreamed even bigger.

Sure, sometimes it can feel uncomfortable to commit to big dreams on paper. But it's important to let your imagination run wild and think up all the amazing ideas of what your life could be and hold. I'm so excited for all your dreams to take flight, and for the wild and wonderful ideas you'll explore – and I wish I had this book as a guide when I was starting out.

Whether you want to get the most out of your personal life, your career or your business, the insights into 'dreaming and doing' in this book may be your most important learnings this year. Be prepared for an amazing adventure!

So, find a quiet place, light a candle, grab a cup of your favourite tea – or do whatever you need to feel comfortable – and let's start dreaming together.

HOW TO GET THE MOST VALUE
FROM THIS BOOK

I recommend that you approach this book step by step. Read each chapter thoroughly. Re-read if you need to. Then do the exercises at the end of each chapter before moving to the next.

Take your time with each chapter. We're all so different, but my estimate is that on average each chapter will take you about an hour to complete – including the reading and the doing. Some may take longer, all depending on how deeply you challenge yourself and the pace you want to go at.

I recommend you do one chapter per week and give yourself lots of time during that week to reflect on the content and the work you've done. My experience is that doing work on yourself like this prompts lots of thoughts and ideas for days afterwards, giving you the chance to refine things as you think about them.

Consider involving your partner, other family members or like-minded friends in the process of reading and working through the book – or even just some of the exercises. I've found it so rewarding – and fun – to work with others on dreaming over the years.

WHERE TO DO
THE WRITTEN EXERCISES

Putting pen to paper and working through the exercises at the end of each chapter is where you will get the most value from this book. Reading is one way of learning, but absorbing yourself in doing the exercises will take you to a whole new level and have the most positive impact on your life.

You'll find the exercises stimulating, fun, challenging, exhilarating and sometimes perhaps confronting. But your dream life lies somewhere beyond your comfort zone.

I recommend that you use the kikki.K Dream Life Journal we've designed specifically to accompany this book. This includes all the worksheets and space you need for your work at the end of each chapter, making the process really simple and easy for you. It's available from kikki.K stores and via www.kikki-k.com.

If you want to get started on some exercises right away, you'll find some downloadable worksheets that you can print yourself at www.kikki-k.com/bookresources.

Another option is to use a journal or notebook of your own. If you do, make sure it's a new one with plenty of pages so you can keep all your work in the one place – easy to find when you need it and to look back on.

For simplicity, as we work through all of the inspiring exercises ahead, I'll refer to the journal you use to do your exercises as your 'Dream Life Journal'.

THERE IS NO PASSION TO BE FOUND

PLAYING SMALL - IN SETTLING FOR

A LIFE THAT IS LESS THAN THE ONE

YOU ARE CAPABLE OF LIVING.

- NELSON MANDELA -

CHAPTER ONE

OPEN YOUR HEART
AND DREAM WITHOUT LIMITS

YOUR DREAM LIFE STARTS HERE

101 DREAMS
INDEX

1 LIVE A HEALTHY LIFE UNTIL I'M
120 YEARS OLD
2 OPEN A KIKKI.K FLAGSHIP STORE IN
NEW YORK CITY
3 TAKE A YEAR OFF WHEN I'M 50

4 INSPIRE AND EMPOWER 101 MILLION PEOPLE TO
WRITE 3 DREAMS DOWN AND START TAKING ACTION TO
5 MAKE THEM COME TRUE

6 DESIGN AND BUILD OUR OWN DREAM HOME

7 BECOME A YOGA TEACHER

8 TAKE TWO WEEKS OFF TO JUST READ, THINK
AND DREAM
9 GIVE A BRILLIANT SPEECH AT AXEL'S 50TH
ON 11TH OF MARCH 2058

10 HAVE AFTERNOON TEA WITH OPRAH IN
HER HOME
11 GO HORSE RIDING FOR A WEEK IN ICELAND
ON ICELANDIC HORSES
12 ATTEND A HEALTH RETREAT EVERY YEAR

13 DANCE WITH PAN AT TIFFANY'S WEDDING

14 SEE BENJAMIN ZANDER CONDUCT IN
BOSTON
15 GO ON AN AFRICAN SAFARI WITH THE
FAMILY
16 RUN A 5K FUN RUN WITH AXEL

17 READ 300 BOOKS IN ONE YEAR

18 COOK A MEAL WITH JAMIE OLIVER

19 TAKE MY WHOLE FAMILY TO THE
MALDIVES
20 WRITE AT LEAST 10 BOOKS!

WHAT WOULD YOU DO IF YOU KNEW YOU COULD NOT FAIL? WHAT WOULD YOU DO WITH YOUR LIFE IF YOU HAD ALL THE TIME AND MONEY YOU NEEDED?

These two questions are my absolute favourites so I'm excited that we're starting this dream journey together with them. Both have something magical about them that get you out of your head and into your heart, where you'll find the most amazing ideas.

If I just asked you simply to write down your dreams, without giving any context, you're likely to write a list of dreams that feel comfortable and achievable, limited by many different factors in your life right now – things like time, money, knowledge and your current circumstances.

All too often, the beliefs we have about what is possible have also been limited by our upbringing and the expectations of others around us.

But if I ask you, 'What would you do if you knew you could not fail? What would you do with your life if you had all the time and money you needed?' this takes you to another level altogether – giving you permission to cast off the constraints of everyday life and to dream big. To reimagine what is possible for you.

There is so much freedom and power in taking time to dream like this, and these two questions are where I start every time I dream – which I do regularly, in the same way many people practise a sport, hobby or music. It helps me to forget about barriers and to let go of limitations. It takes me to places and gives me ideas I never would have without this approach. It's literally life transforming – and it's so, so simple.

I truly believe that dreaming is the first step to creating your dream life. There's something so special about giving yourself the time and space just to dream – to imagine how your life could be. When dreaming becomes a part of your everyday life, it becomes life changing.

I'm convinced that a key reason everyone in the world doesn't practise regular dreaming in a structured way is because they're unaware of the enormous benefits it will bring their way.

I remember when, sometime not long after writing my 3am List, I attended a seminar as part of my journey to find 'my thing' in life. One of the speakers briefly mentioned the idea of practising dreaming without limitation. A light bulb went off in my mind. I hadn't thought of dreaming before as a practice, like meditating or yoga, and I hadn't contemplated the idea – or experienced the power – of regularly dreaming without limitations.

Soon after, I took time out to reflect on my 3am List and, for the first time in my life, I sat down and took time to practise dreaming completely without limitations. I asked myself the first question I asked you: What would I do if I knew I couldn't fail? I began to write down a list of everything that bubbled up for me. They were big dreams, far beyond my normal thinking, and it was so exciting to see them take shape on paper – almost as if they had a life of their own.

When I scribbled on my list a dream that felt like 'the one', I was almost too excited to keep writing. It gave me goosebumps. My heart pumped fast.

IT WAS A DREAM SO BIG AND SO EXCITING FOR ME THAT I RUSHED HOME TO PAUL AND SQUEALED, 'I KNOW EXACTLY WHAT I'M GOING TO DO WITH MY LIFE. I'M GOING TO OPEN BEAUTIFUL SWEDISH DESIGN AND STATIONERY STORES IN ALL MY FAVOURITE CITIES AROUND THE WORLD! LONDON, PARIS, TOKYO, NEW YORK, STOCKHOLM, HONG KONG…' AS I KEPT LISTING CITIES, PAUL LOOKED AT ME WITH A TOUCH OF SHOCK, WHICH SOON TURNED INTO A KNOWING LOOK OF SHARED EXCITEMENT.

I felt so certain about that dream – more certain than I'd felt about anything before in my life. I had no idea whether or not it could be done (which turned out to be a blessing – ignorance can be bliss), but I knew I had to try. That dream, of course, was the start of kikki.K – my global stationery and design business – with the name coming later over a few glasses of wine with friends, combining my childhood nickname 'kikki' and 'K' from my surname, Karlsson.

Dreaming is something I've now studied and incorporated into my life on a regular basis – it's one of the most important things I spend time on – and I want to inspire and empower you to do the same. I'm certain that, once you start, it will ignite a spark in you that will fire such a strong sense of possibility and excitement for your future that you'll never be quite the same. A door will open that you won't be able to close.

So, whether you're feeling a little lost like I was, feeling like something is missing in your life, or even if you feel clear about where you want to go and you want to stretch yourself further, dreaming is the perfect place to start. It's your first step towards shaping an amazing future for yourself and your loved ones – and creating positive ripples that will flow to your community and the world.

While dreaming is such a big part of my life, I'm always surprised by how few people make time to dream regularly. It's not something taught in schools – as far as I know – and my experience is that most people don't teach their children the process either. I wish this were different! What an amazing and positive impact this will have on the world when we all do it.

Once you've learnt how, this one habit will be something that opens new doors, changes your perspective, brings new opportunities and is, without doubt, the key to you creating your dream life, whatever that means for you now and at different times through the years ahead.

Your dreams can be big or small. They might take years or just days to achieve. It doesn't matter. It's all about letting your dreams come to life, and falling in love with the feelings of excitement and possibility that they create. Just starting this process will open a door in your mind and you'll be surprised by how often possibilities and ideas will bubble up, often at unexpected times.

After going through the process of brainstorming and writing down any dreams you can think of on paper, it's quite amazing how you'll start to consciously and subconsciously take steps to make them come true. Dreams have such power to pull you forward. It's even more powerful when you share them with like-minded people, who you'll find will often help you in big and small ways to achieve those dreams.

I find it so inspiring to hear other people's dreams, so in case you feel the same way, here's a sneak peek at some of my 101 Dreams.

A SNEAK PEEK INTO MY 101 DREAMS JOURNAL

+ LIVE A HEALTHY LIFE UNTIL I'M 120 YEARS OLD
+ OPEN A KIKKI.K FLAGSHIP STORE IN NEW YORK CITY
+ TAKE A YEAR OFF WHEN I TURN FIFTY – LONG WAY AWAY BUT PLANNING IT IS FUN!
+ INSPIRE AND EMPOWER 101 MILLION PEOPLE TO WRITE DOWN THREE DREAMS AND START TAKING ACTION TO MAKE THEM COME TRUE
+ DESIGN AND BUILD OUR OWN DREAM HOME
+ BECOME A PART-TIME YOGA TEACHER
+ TAKE TWO WEEKS OFF EVERY YEAR JUST TO READ AND THINK
+ HAVE AFTERNOON TEA WITH OPRAH IN HER HOME AND DISCUSS HOW WE CAN INSPIRE PEOPLE THE WORLD OVER TO DREAM
+ GIVE A BRILLIANT SPEECH AT MY SON AXEL'S FIFTIETH ON 11TH MARCH 2058 (I'LL NEED TO STAY HEALTHY AND WELL!)
+ GO HORSE RIDING FOR A WEEK IN ICELAND ON ICELANDIC HORSES
+ ATTEND A HEALTH RETREAT EVERY YEAR

These aren't all dreams that I'm working on right now, but they're there in my 101 Dreams Journal. I glance over them often and I'll start working towards each whenever the time is right for me. I add to my list regularly and my intention is to keep adding to it my entire life.

Soon you'll start your own 101 Dreams List and you can add to it whenever you come up with a new dream.

You'll need to make sure you can give yourself at least thirty minutes – preferably an hour – in a quiet and inspiring place. Choose somewhere you'll be comfortable and won't be interrupted. I always like to pour myself a cup of my favourite tea, light a candle, and pull out my beautiful journal and pen. I start by centring myself, taking three deep breaths and then I remind myself that I only have one life, and I want to make every day and month and year count. Then I work through the following exercise.

I'm going to ask you a series of questions and I'd love you to write whatever comes to mind on the 101 Dreams List on the following pages or in your Dream Life Journal. When you're finished writing every dream you can think of on the page, read back through the questions again and then go back to your list and keep writing whatever comes to mind.

Write down as many dreams as you can in the time you give yourself, and come back and do this powerful exercise as often as you like over the course of your life. I'd suggest doing this every few months, but do it at least annually.

The idea is to just get as many dreams down on paper as you possibly can. Later when you reflect on them, some will totally inspire you. Some will inspire completely new dreams you hadn't thought of before. Some you will edit. Some you may later throw away...

But somewhere on that list will be some absolute gems that will ignite your soul and inspire you to reimagine your life in ways you wouldn't have otherwise.

Be as bold as you like. Be as silly as you like. Be as childish as you like.

You are about to start reimagining and reshaping your future. How exciting!

DREAM GUIDANCE

To help you get started, here is what I share with people about dreaming. Read through it as many times as you like as you do this practice. A good alternative is to listen to my 101 Dreams Guide as you write – many people find the verbal prompts, inspiration and guidance help them get the most from the experience and it's really useful to play in the background if you're dreaming with others (www.kikki-k.com/bookresources).

Immerse yourself in your inspiring space where you won't be interrupted. When you're ready, close your eyes while you take three slow, deep breaths. This is your time. Open your eyes when you're done.

Don't worry about the doing. Don't filter what you come up with. Don't worry about sorting through them. Just connect with your heart, dream big and capture those dreams on paper as quickly, roughly and simply as you like. Think of this as a brainstorming exercise.

I want you to imagine your life without any limitations. You have all the money you need. Time is no limit. There is no urgency. No musts. No shoulds. And you cannot fail.

Imagine you can do whatever you want to do and have whatever you want to have. To be whoever you want to be.

You are not constrained at all by what your parents think, what your friends think, what your partner thinks, what anyone thinks. You are totally free to just be you – to be your best self and to dream without any limitations about what you want for yourself, for those you love and care about, and for the world.

I'm giving you permission to stop for a moment and just let go of everything you thought you could or couldn't do. The world is so full of possibilities. It all starts with a dream, so this is your turn to cast all doubts and all constraints aside and give yourself the gift of dreaming. Dream away.

Now, let's put pen to paper and use the questions ahead to inspire, prompt and guide you to create your own list of 101 Dreams – or as many as you can. As they surface in your mind, write those dreams onto your 101 Dreams List. You can edit later.

Read each question in the three areas on the opposite page one by one. After reading each question, pause, think about that question, and let it stimulate your imagination. When you've written down every dream it inspires, move to the next question, and so on.

When you feel you're out of ideas, cycle through the three lists of questions again. Do this as many times as you like to inspire as many dreams as you possibly can. Let your imagination run wild. Tap your creativity. And remember, turn off your rational mind. Resist the temptation to limit yourself.

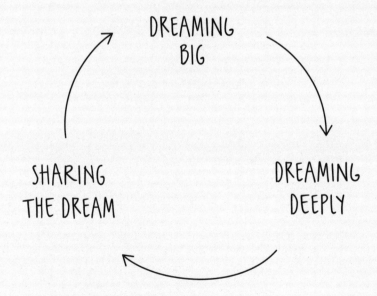

DREAMING
BIG

DREAMING
DEEPLY

SHARING
THE DREAM

EXERCISE

01 / DREAMING BIG

+ WHAT WOULD YOU DO IF YOU KNEW YOU COULD NOT FAIL?

+ WHAT WOULD YOU DO IF YOU HAD ALL THE MONEY AND TIME YOU NEEDED?

+ WHAT WOULD YOU DO IF YOU HAD ALL THE SKILLS AND KNOWLEDGE YOU NEEDED?

+ WHAT WOULD YOU DO IF YOU HAD ALL THE COURAGE YOU NEEDED, ALL THE SELF-BELIEF YOU NEEDED?

+ WHAT WOULD YOU DO IF YOU HAD ALL THE SUPPORT YOU NEEDED?

+ WHAT DREAMS DO YOU HAVE ALREADY?

+ WHAT HAVE YOU OFTEN WISHED FOR, BUT NEVER PUT IN WRITING?

+ WHAT HAVE YOU DREAMED ABOUT, BUT NEVER SHARED WITH ANYONE ELSE?

---

02 / DREAMING DEEPLY

LOOK DEEPLY INTO YOUR HEART, AND CONSIDER THE FOLLOWING QUESTIONS TOO.
THINK ABOUT YOUR DREAM LIFE AND HOW IT WOULD BE DIFFERENT TO YOUR LIFE TODAY...

+ WHAT WOULD YOU START DOING?

+ WHAT WOULD YOU STOP DOING?

+ HOW WOULD YOU SPEND YOUR TIME?

+ WHAT WOULD YOU DO FOR WORK?

+ WHAT EXPERIENCES WOULD YOU HAVE?

+ WHERE WOULD YOU TRAVEL?

+ WHAT WOULD YOU BUY?

+ WHAT WOULD YOUR PURPOSE BE?

+ WHERE WOULD YOU LIVE?

+ WHAT WOULD YOU SURROUND YOURSELF WITH?

+ HOW WOULD YOU FEEL AND ACT?

---

03 / SHARING THE DREAM

IF YOUR LIFE WAS FILLED WITH ALL THE LOVE AND DEEPLY SATISFYING RELATIONSHIPS YOU COULD HOPE FOR, HOW WOULD IT LOOK?

+ WHO WOULD BE THE KEY PEOPLE IN YOUR DREAM LIFE? DESCRIBE YOUR RELATIONSHIPS WITH THEM IN JUST A FEW WORDS...

+ WHAT DREAMS DO YOU HAVE TO HELP YOUR LOVED ONES – YOUR FAMILY, YOUR FRIENDS?

+ WHAT DO YOU DREAM OF FOR YOUR COMMUNITY? FOR THE WORLD?

MY 101 DREAMS

01 _____

02 _____

03 _____

04 _____

05 _____

06 _____

07 _____

08 _____

09 _____

10 _____

11 _____

12 _____

13 _____

14 _____

15 _____

16 _____

17 _____

18 _____

19 _____

20 _____

21 _____

22 _____

23 _____

24 _____

25 _____

26 _____

27 _____

28 _____

29 _____

30 _____

31 _____

32 _____

33 _____

34 _____

35 _____

36 _____

37 _____

38 _____

39 _____

40 _____

41 _____

42 _____

43 _____

44 _____

45 _____

46 _____

47 _____

48 _____

49 _____

50 _____

51 _____

52 _____

53 _____

54 _____

55 _____

56 _____

57 _____

58 _____

59 _____

60 _____

61 _____

62 _____

63 _____

64 _____

65 _____

66 _____

67 _____

68 _____

69 _____

70 _____

71 _____

72 _____

73 _____

74 _____

75 _____

76 _____

77 _____

78 _____

79 _____

80 _____

81 _____

82 _____

83 _____

84 _____

85 _____

86 _____

87 _____

88 _____

89 _____

90 _____

91 _____

92 _____

93 _____

94 _____

95 _____

96 _____

97 _____

98 _____

99 _____

100 _____

101 _____

OPEN YOUR HEART AND DREAM WITHOUT LIMITS

1 DREAMING IS THE FIRST STEP
TO CREATING AND LIVING
YOUR DREAM LIFE

2 IN ORDER TO DREAM BIG, YOU
HAVE TO ASK YOURSELF THE
RIGHT QUESTIONS TO HELP
YOU LET GO OF LIMITATIONS

3 DON'T WORRY ABOUT THE
DOING YET – JUST GIVE
YOURSELF PERMISSION TO
DREAM AND TO CAPTURE
THOSE DREAMS ON PAPER

CHAPTER TWO

BE INSPIRED BY THE DREAMS OF OTHERS

YOUR DREAM LIFE STARTS HERE

So much of our experience in life comes from the people we meet and the people we surround ourselves with. People are an amazing source of inspiration and hearing about their dreams is one of the most powerful ways of inspiring you to pursue your dream life too.

Meeting people in real life is a wonderful way of learning from them, but I also love to spend hours reading and watching documentaries about people from all walks of life who have chased and achieved their dreams – big and small.

I love asking people about their dreams and I especially love being in a room full of people sharing their dreams. It's so special, and I always walk away inspired with new ideas for dreams I personally want to chase.

Given my interest in growing a meaningful organisation, I particularly love meeting entrepreneurs from around the globe and find it so interesting to hear their stories and dreams – their achievements and learnings. I'm a member of the global Entrepreneurs' Organization (EO), which brings me into regular contact with people from many different countries doing all sorts of amazing things. For me, that's super inspiring. I also go out of my way to meet and surround myself in my work with lots of creative people – people doing interesting and meaningful things to inspire others in their communities and in the world. Do you surround yourself with people who inspire you too?

I find it fascinating to hear what people want to achieve, and this often sets me on pathways to new dreams that I would never have thought of myself. This is why it's so exciting to ask people outside your own circle about their dreams. There's something so lovely about bringing other people into your dreaming too, particularly those you love. Consider involving your partner, your children, your parents, your colleagues. I particularly love imagining and dreaming with my partner and my children, who often surprise me with dreams that we add to our long family 101 Dreams List. Stop for a moment and think about how you could do that...

A friend of mine, who had recently done the dreaming exercise from the previous chapter, shared with me the following, '...I asked my husband the question, "What would you do if you knew you could not fail?" His answer surprised me so much ... and we've been together ten years. He said he would become a politician and change the world for our children! He is such a quiet, reserved man that this was very unexpected.'

I love that story. My friend's husband may or may not become a politician, but maybe that has planted the seed of an idea for him. Maybe that will lead to him joining his children's school council, or the committee of a sporting or other group the children are involved in so he can influence that part of their world. The point is, contemplating the question and dreaming without constraint caused a shift in his thinking. Who knows where it could lead? Maybe sharing your dreaming with your partner will surprise you too.

Back to meeting people to inspire you ... I make a list of all the people I want to meet (and you'll do the same at the end of this chapter), but I don't think about how I can meet them – that comes later. Simply by writing down their names, you are more likely to be aware of opportunities to meet them or learn more about them. And it's surprising how often it works.

Take, for example, Sir Richard Branson. When I started my business, I read some fantastic books he had written and I put him on my list of people I really wanted to meet. Quite a few years later, over the span of a couple of weeks, I ran into a couple of people who had met Richard. Then I read an article about someone who had been to his home on Necker Island in the Caribbean and, to top it off, shortly afterwards I received an invitation to visit Necker Island to be part of a conference he was hosting. I realised it was a brilliant learning opportunity, so I went.

All quite coincidental, but even if you put a name on the list and you feel it's highly unlikely you'll ever have the chance to meet that person, don't worry about that now. Just dream big and add names, and think about how to make it happen later. The opportunity just may come up one day or you might be able to find a way to make it happen.

Another example of me doing this was with Arianna Huffington – an inspiring woman you'll read about later in this book. I was lucky enough to meet her in New York and we've since gone on to collaborate on a kikki.K product range (designed around her million-plus-selling book, *Thrive*).

Similarly, I'd always admired Stella McCartney – particularly how driven by her values she is – and had put her name on my list. After thinking through all the people in the UK who might share my passion for inspiring the world to dream, I remembered having Stella on that list and so I found a way to meet her for a cup of tea. Meeting people like this has been incredibly inspiring for me. I love adding people to my dreams list, and it's growing every day.

Your list could be made up of people you know and admire, or people a bit more remote, like a famous entrepreneur or an author who inspires you. To learn more about them and be inspired by their dreams and what they do, you could go along to see them speak at an event or book signing or read about them online.

With Arianna, she was just starting Thrive Global – an organisation she created to help people lower stress and enhance their wellbeing and performance – so there was a natural fit for us to collaborate (although I didn't know that when I first wrote her name on my list of people to meet). I asked around if people knew her, but in the end I just contacted her directly. It always seems impossible until it's done.

Another was a person I admire from the retail industry who had followed his dreams and built a wonderful business. I heard him speak at an event and afterwards I went up and asked if he was free to meet for a coffee. He later became a mentor for me.

It's important to seize every chance you can to hear about the dreams of others. When I'm sharing a meal with people, I'll often ask them to share a dream, and the conversation that follows always takes the experience to a whole new level and connects people in new and deeper ways. And it's always fun.

I know some people find it a little awkward at first to ask a question like this – thinking it might sound a little deep or maybe even a little intrusive. That's simply because it's not yet so normal and natural for them. Let's face it, it's often only at weddings and similar events, or in songs, that people talk in public about their hopes, aspirations and dreams. Now that's something we need to change!

NO MATTER WHERE YOU'RE FROM,

YOUR DREAMS ARE VALID.

- LUPITA NYONG'O -

Why don't you give it a try next time you gather with your friends, family or colleagues? Break the ice by sharing that you're reading a book about the power of dreaming, that you love hearing other people's dreams and you'd love to hear any dreams they have for themselves. Maybe even read them some of the real-life dreams of people you'll soon get to see on the following pages.

Then share a dream or two of yours and ask them to share any they have. Be confident in your belief that dreaming matters.

Recently, I did a 101 Dreams exercise with my lovely book group, and I got so many ideas to expand my dreams as I listened to theirs. And I later learnt that others in the group were subsequently inspired to do the exercise with their families and friends. One of my friends, Anna-Carin, was so inspired she did it with a group of her colleagues, who, in turn, were so inspired and got so much value from it that they've planned to do it together at least every year. I love that ripple effect of people inspiring each other to reimagine their future by dreaming! And that's what I want to spread across the world, to create positive change for millions...

It's a good idea to do this annually with a group of people and create your own dream group.

Why not partner up with a friend or friends to read this book, do the exercises, and then meet up to share your progress and ideas? In my experience, everyone involved will get amazing value from the experience. Give it some thought.

I particularly love getting groups of like-minded people together to share dreams and the progress we're all making, and I'm really proud that our stores and social channels are now becoming hubs for like-minded people to gather and share.

Imagine the power and positive outcomes if school classes, workplaces, teams, communities or even nations came together regularly and effectively to create, share and chase dreams.

Later in our journey together we'll go deeper into the concept of sharing dreams and how sharing your own dreams with others can be amazingly powerful, but for now let's just explore how you can be inspired by the dreams of others.

EXERCISE

THIS CHAPTER'S EXERCISES ARE SIMPLE.

01 /

IN THE TABLE ON THE FOLLOWING SPREAD OR IN YOUR DREAM LIFE JOURNAL, CREATE A LIST OF
PEOPLE YOU'D LOVE TO MEET. IT COULD BE SOMEONE YOU SIMPLY ADMIRE OR IT COULD BE SOMEONE
WHO'S DONE SOMETHING YOU REALLY WANT TO DO ONE DAY. YOU CAN WRITE A SPECIFIC NAME
OR YOU CAN EVEN JUST WRITE 'SOMEONE WHO CAN SHARE THEIR EXPERIENCE ON X, Y AND Z' AND
WORK OUT LATER WHO THAT PERSON COULD BE. START WITH AIMING FOR TEN PEOPLE AND, OVER
YOUR LIFETIME, I'D LOVE YOU TO AIM FOR 101 PEOPLE. THIS MIGHT SOUND LIKE A LOT, BUT IT'S
WORTH AIMING HIGH. ADD TO YOUR LIST AS OTHERS COME TO MIND. IN MY EXPERIENCE, THE MORE
YOU DO THIS, THE MORE PEOPLE YOU WILL WANT TO MEET.

TO START THIS LIST, PUT A TIMER ON FOR THREE MINUTES AND WRITE AS MANY AS YOU CAN THINK OF
BEFORE PAUSING.

NOW SET YOUR TIMER FOR TEN MINUTES AND KEEP ADDING TO YOUR LIST. GET BRAVER AND BOLDER.
THINK BIGGER. KEEP WRITING UNTIL YOU'RE DONE.

MAKE A NOTE IN YOUR DIARY TO COME BACK LATER IN THE WEEK TO RE-READ AND ADD MORE NAMES
TO YOUR LIST. PUT A NOTE IN YOUR DIARY TO DO THE EXERCISE AGAIN, ANNUALLY AT LEAST.

---

02 /

WHEN YOU'VE FINISHED BRAINSTORMING NAMES, GO BACK THROUGH YOUR LIST AND FILL IN THE
ANSWERS IN THE COLUMNS TO THE RIGHT: WHY DO YOU WANT TO MEET THEM? WHAT CAN YOU
LEARN FROM THEM? WHAT WOULD YOU GET OUT OF LEARNING THAT FROM THEM? HOW COULD
YOU MEET THEM? IF ANY OF THEIR DREAMS OR ACHIEVEMENTS INSPIRE YOU, ADD THOSE TO YOUR
OWN 101 DREAMS LIST.

---

03 /

READ THROUGH THE VARIOUS DREAMS WE'VE ASSEMBLED ON THE FOLLOWING PAGES - THEY'RE FROM
FROM MY KIKKI.K TEAM AND THEIR FAMILIES, OUR GUESTS (THAT'S WHAT WE CALL OUR CUSTOMERS),
PEOPLE I KNOW, SOME OF THE MANY PEOPLE I MEET AROUND THE WORLD WHO SHARE THEIR DREAMS
WITH ME AND OTHERS. SOME OF THEM SHARED ANONYMOUSLY. AGAIN, IF ANY OF THEM INSPIRE IDEAS
FOR DREAMS FOR YOU, THEN ADD THEM TO YOUR 101 DREAMS LIST.

EXERCISE

04 /

OVER THE NEXT WEEK, ASK THE PEOPLE IN YOUR LIFE – YOUR FAMILY, PARTNER, CHILDREN, FRIENDS, COLLEAGUES – WHAT THEIR DREAMS ARE AND WHAT THEIR DREAM LIFE WOULD LOOK LIKE FOR THEM IF THEY WERE TO STOP AND THINK ABOUT IT, WITHOUT ANY LIMITS. BE GENUINELY CURIOUS AND SEE IF YOU CAN FIND SOME MORE INSPIRATION IN THE DREAMS OF OTHERS. AND WHO KNOWS, YOU JUST MIGHT INSPIRE THEM GREATLY BY DOING THAT – WHICH IS WHAT HAPPENED IN THE AMAZING TRUE STORY OF DR TERERAI TRENT THAT YOU'LL READ AT THE END OF THIS CHAPTER.

---

05 /

IMAGINE SETTING UP A DREAM GROUP, LIKE A BOOK GROUP. THINK ABOUT LIKE-MINDED PEOPLE YOU COULD INVITE AND MAKE A LIST OF THEM. ACT ON THIS IF IT FEELS RIGHT FOR YOU.

---

06 /

MAKE THESE EXERCISES PART OF THE RHYTHM OF YOUR LIFE: CHOOSE A TIME TO REPEAT THEM YEARLY, MAKING SURE TO NOTE WHEN TO DO THEM IN YOUR DIARY SO YOU'RE REMINDED WHEN YOU NEED TO BE AND CAN FREE YOUR MIND. **CULTIVATE A DAILY OPENNESS TO ASKING OTHERS ABOUT THEIR DREAMS AND BEING INSPIRED BY THE DREAMS OF OTHERS.**

---

07 /

FOR ONGOING INSPIRATION FROM THE DREAMS AND STORIES OF OTHERS, SUBSCRIBE TO MY PODCASTS AND BLOG VIA WWW.KIKKI-K.COM/DREAMLIFE AND FOLLOW THE HASHTAGS #KIKKIKDREAMLIFE AND #101MILLIONDREAMERS. LATER IN THE BOOK WE'LL BE ENCOURAGING YOU TO SHARE YOUR DREAMS WITH OTHERS, IF THAT FEELS RIGHT FOR YOU GIVEN YOUR PERSONAL CIRCUMSTANCES.

101 PEOPLE I WANT TO MEET

	WHO	WHY I WANT TO MEET THEM
01		
02		
03		
04	Anthoy Horowitz	
05		
06		
07		
08		
09		
10		
11		
12		
13		
14		
15		
16		
17		
18		
19		
20		

101 PEOPLE I WANT TO MEET

WHAT I CAN LEARN FROM THEM	WHAT I WOULD GET OUT OF LEARNING THAT FROM THEM	HOW I COULD MEET THEM

IF YOU HAVEN'T FOUND IT YET,

KEEP LOOKING. DON'T SETTLE. AS

WITH ALL MATTERS OF THE HEART,

YOU'LL KNOW WHEN YOU FIND IT.

– STEVE JOBS –

REAL DREAMS YOU MAY FIND INSPIRING

+ 'My dream is to live healthily in every way to 100 years of age.' – Sue, 43

+ 'A dream of mine is to dance with my daughter at her wedding. I might be in my seventies by then so I need to be healthy, fit and agile!' – Paul, 50

+ 'I'm dreaming that they'll find a matching organ donor for me and that I'll have a successful transplant, get back to normal health and be around for my family.'

+ 'My dream is to have children and be an awesome mother one day.'

+ 'A dream is to document in film the story of our family history, particularly of the generation who experienced the two world wars, so the many learnings will benefit future generations.'

+ 'A dream of mine is that my children will one day consider me among the best men they ever met.'

+ 'My dream is to have my own successful business that allows me to work from wherever I like in the world so that I can do as much travelling as possible. I also dream to be an amazing mother and wife one day, travelling the world with my family and experiencing fantastic things.' – Katie

+ 'My BIG Dream is to create gourmet home-cooked meals for dogs and deliver fresh, wholesome meals to pet lovers all over my local area.' – Misty

+ 'Use my skills/experience to make myself indispensable to an organisation I love working with – and a team I love working with – where I know my work has true meaning and my career can thrive.' – Kerry

+ 'I dream of being able to find a way to get lots of help so our home feels clean and tidy more often without me having to be on it all the time and so we can have more quality family time together while the children still live at home.'

+ 'A dream of mine is to mentor ten young children through to their teens – those who live in dysfunctional family homes and just need a bit of support, encouragement and guidance the way I did.'

+ 'I dream of being able to send my children to a great university one day...'

+ *'To create regular space in our lives where my husband and I can spend quality time together without the rush and demands of everyday life.'*

+ *'I'm dreaming of opening my own café – healthy food and great coffee.'*

+ *'My dream is to make a living vlogging on YouTube.'* – Axel (axelkl), 10

+ *'My dream is to go to New York one day with my mum and see the American Girl doll store.'* – Tiffany, 7

+ *'Take a year off and travel the world – and learn what I can about how we can solve our many environmental challenges.'*

+ *'My dream is to realise the dream of my younger self: "to be like a mentor to deaf children when I am older and can do it". I didn't know then that I would also be going blind. My younger self also wanted me to write books on how to be a special friend to a special child.'* – Kate

+ *'My dream is to finish my degree in psychology and become a school psychologist. I want to be able to listen and guide the children who need it and those who just need a chat. Sometimes that's all someone needs to help change their mindframe.'* – Laura

+ *'My dream is to be in a position in life where I can make decisions based on what I want, not what my financial situation, society or family tell me to.'* – Georgia

+ *'My dream is to be a career consultant for young women. I want to help them recognise their passion, power and talents so they make the best career choices that they can.'* – Marin

+ *'My dream is to truly live in the present. I spend so much time planning the future or thinking about the past that I forget the present. So I dream to have the power to be present every day and actually enjoy life more.'* – Charlotte

+ *'My dream is to help stop bullying and to teach young people about respecting themselves and what they have been through.'* – Shannen

+ *'For my passion/business to earn enough for me to go full-time and quit the office job. Slowly chipping away at making that dream a reality.'* – Kimberly

+ *'My dream is for there one day to be no wars or fighting of any sort on earth. I'm thirteen years old, so I hope in my lifetime I will see my dream come true.'* – Monique

+ *'I dream to one day have breakfast with the giraffes at the Giraffe Manor in Africa after an amazing safari.'*

- *'My dream is to nurse in a paediatric hospital on Christmas Day, to make the day exceptionally special and make children smile through a difficult time.'*

- *'My dream would be to go to Denmark to the Happiness Institute and meet Mike Weiking and discuss all things happy while eating pastry.'*

- *'My dream is to open up a rescue centre for all animals, every shape, every size, and to never have to turn away an animal in need.'*

- *'To own my own business that makes a positive difference to my community, and to be a role model to my daughter. I want her to see me practise the importance of having ambition, working hard, chasing dreams, but also taking time off and prioritising health and giggles with family.'*

- *'To be a music therapist, spread the power of music, cure people with it.'*

- *'To grow my business to a point where I feel fulfilled and have enough money to spoil my family and thank them for all they have done for me.'*

- *'To live beside a beach and walk my dogs on it every day.'*

- *'One of my biggest dreams is to buy a place, renovate it and live in it!'*

- *'To own a summer place in Sweden, close to my parents to make it easier for us to visit every year and also to have something to pass on to my children to help keep their strong connection with my heritage once I am gone.'* – Jen

- *'One of my dreams is to enjoy a traditional British Christmas with my family back in the UK. Then to travel north to welcome the new year in Edinburgh with Iain's Scottish family. And then to Finland to spend time with my family before heading north to see the Northern Lights in Lapland. So excited!!!!!!'* – Sue

- *'Sell my home-grown organic fruit and vegetables at farmers' markets out of a small vintage caravan called "Ollie, the Organic Van".'* – Lil

- *'Open a retreat on my five-acre farm specifically for families going through hardship with their children in hospital (a home away from home) just as we did staying at Ronald McDonald House when our twins had heart surgeries.'* – Rebecca

- *'To travel to New York, stay at a beautiful hotel, do the High Line walk, eat at ABC Cocina and visit the MoMA museum.'* – Mel

- *'Compete in a triathlon (just started adult swimming lessons!).'* – Nicole

- *'After seeing the exhibition "Monet's Garden" with my mother, I have dreamt about being able to take her to his garden in Giverny, France, that inspired so many of his masterpieces, to see this beautiful place together.'*

- *'To visit the cherry blossom trees in Japan as my grandfather told me "they were out of this world to behold". He visited them while he was stationed in Japan after the Second World War.'*

- *'See the Northern Lights.'*

- *'To take Hanna to New York for her thirteenth birthday.'* – Jen

- *'Make a big positive impact on someone else's life.'*

- *'My dream is fairly simple ... it's to live a life full of love, happiness and health, so that I can better the lives of people around me.'*

- *'My dream is to do something that involves sharing information, ensuring people are better off today than they were yesterday, and empowering people (and businesses) to take control. I had a light bulb moment and realised that OHS consulting was for me.'* – Lisa

- *'I love singing. I like sharing the songs that inspire me with others. My dream is to hold a live concert with friends who have the same dream.'*

- *'My dream is simple. To own my story, to be in the driving seat of my own life. To overcome the things holding me back.'*

- *'My dream is to one day own a restaurant. I have recently found a passion for cooking beautiful food and I would love to open a business venture where I can inspire people with wonderful food, as well as create a place for people to come together.'* – Rose

- *'My dream is not to have to work for money. To be financially free!'* – Mable

- *'My dream is to travel the world researching and writing about food, to expand people's knowledge about different cultures and cuisines. Food is a huge connector and I believe exposing people to different cuisines is a great way to bridge our differences and celebrate our similarities.'* – Vic

- *'My dream is to be a coach for women who struggle to find the confidence and drive to take action on their dreams.'* – Alana

- *'One of my biggest dreams is to take a year off work to travel – or the ultimate dream – having a job that allows me to work remotely so I can travel as much as I can!'* – Britt

- 'My dream is to complete the four-part book series I've been working on since 1999 based on music my sister wrote for piano. I am currently half way through book three.' – Jason

- 'My dream is to see my mother beat her battle with cancer and to be able to take my parents on the cruise they have always wanted to go on.' – Michelle

- 'I dream about building a new home that has a small private extension where my mother can live too. My mother gave me everything that I ever needed in life and if I build this house, I can tempt her to leave the green hills of Ireland and come live with me, at least for a few months each year.' – Leanne

- 'I have a dream where all humans are treated equally – in love, in respect, in wealth, in health, etc. – no matter where they're from. Who knows, we might not be the only humans in the universe.' – Robert

- 'My dream is to become a life coach.'

- 'I dream that when my wife and I are in our twilight years and the boys have grown up and have their own families, we will have amazing Christmases together and celebrate with grandchildren.' – Tony

- 'My dream is to open my own wellness café and yoga studio by the beach on a tropical island.' – Lotus

- 'My lovely husband is in the army and we are on the move every few years – my dream is for us to buy a property in our home state so we can visit our family as often as we'd like, and eventually be able to call that house a home.' – Deanne

- 'I would love to one day live in a foreign country! Even if it's just for a short amount of time, I think it would be an amazing personal and cultural experience.' – Jess

- 'My dream is to one day dance for the National Ballet. Just being able to perform and call myself a member of the company would be a dream come true.'

- 'My big dream is to give my girls (five-year-old and two-year-old) a life full of adventure and purpose. My small dream is to give them daily or weekly adventurous and fun quality time that fills up their love cup.' – Tasha

- 'I have a dream that my four little children will one day live in a nation where they will not be judged by the colour of their skin but by the content of their character.' – Martin Luther King Jr

BE INSPIRED BY THE DREAMS OF OTHERS

1 PEOPLE CAN BE AN AMAZING SOURCE OF INSPIRATION FOR YOUR OWN DREAMS

2 DON'T BE AFRAID TO ASK PEOPLE ABOUT THEIR DREAMS, AND SHARE YOURS TOO: SHARING DREAMS IS ONE OF THE MOST POWERFUL THINGS WE CAN ALL DO

3 CONSIDER PARTNERING WITH A FRIEND OR FRIENDS TO READ THIS BOOK, DO THE EXERCISES AND MEET UP TO SHARE YOUR PROGRESS AND IDEAS

4 WHEN YOU SHARE DREAMS, YOU INSPIRE OTHERS

IF YOU ARE NOT WILLING TO

RISK THE USUAL, YOU WILL HAVE

TO SETTLE FOR THE ORDINARY.

- JIM ROHN -

TINOGONA – IT IS ACHIEVABLE!

DR TERERAI TRENT

Dr Tererai Trent's story of dreaming is, without doubt, the most amazing I have ever come across, and I'm honoured she has allowed me to share it with you here with her blessing. I'll do my best to give you an insight, but you simply have to read and watch more about this incredible woman. Chosen by Oprah Winfrey as her all-time favourite guest EVER, Tererai truly is one of my heroes.

Born in a village in rural Zimbabwe, Tererai went to elementary school only briefly before being sent out to work in the fields of her small community. Each day she tended the family's cattle and fetched water and firewood from many miles away. Sometimes she ran into older boys carrying books on their way to school. She longed to trade her firewood for books. But for most little girls in her village, learning and school were impossible. If families had any money for school, they sent boys. Girls were kept at home to cook, clean and bring supplies.

Undeterred, she still dreamed of an education and convinced her brother to teach her how to read and write. When she was eleven years of age, her father married her off in exchange for a cow – as was traditional in her culture.

'Before I was eighteen, I was already a mother of four,' she said. 'One of the babies died as an infant because I failed to produce enough milk to feed the child. I was a child myself. I realised that the pathway that I was on silenced me. But I wanted an education so badly.'

Like generations of women before her, there seemed no way Tererai would be able to escape her lot in life. Then fate intervened with the arrival of an American woman: Jo Luck, Director of International Programs for a non-profit, Heifer International (and later its President and CEO).

Visiting Tererai's village, Jo Luck stopped at a circle of women sitting around in the dust. She asked them what Tererai calls a fundamental question, 'What are your dreams?' and told them, 'If you believe in your dreams, they are achievable.'

Tererai was one of those women. Feeling too ashamed to speak up, she kept her eyes down, but Jo Luck persisted, 'Young woman, why are you quiet? What are your dreams?' 'And I'm not sure – maybe it was the way she looked at me, or the way she kept nudging me to speak, but I said I want to go to America, I want to get an undergraduate degree, a master's and a doctorate,' Tererai said.

'There was silence, because the other women knew I did not even have a high school diploma. I was twenty, poor, uneducated, living in an abusive relationship and at the time also expecting my fifth child. And this woman looked at me and said, "Tererai, if you believe in your dreams, they are achievable." And she repeated the word, *"tinogona, tinogona"*. In my language that word means *"it is achievable",'* said Tererai.

Inspired by Jo Luck and essentially being given permission to dream, Tererai later scribbled down on a scrap of paper four seemingly impossible dreams. Dreams she knew would help her escape poverty and the demeaning generational cycle that ran deep in her family and community.

Then, her mother told her, 'Your dreams will have more meaning when they are tied to the betterment of your community,' so Tererai wrote a fifth dream. 'When I'm done, I will come back and improve the lives of women and children in my community. I will give the gift of education.'

The final dream added to the list, Tererai buried the scrap of paper in a tin can in the earth of her village, in what was a deeply symbolic gesture for her.

Despite poverty, and a lack of running water and electricity, Tererai comes from a culture rich in its values and rituals, grounded in her people's ancient connections to earth and life wisdom. Both birth and death are celebrated with the same respect through their connection to the earth, and a child's birth is not symbolically complete until a female elder carefully snips a piece of the umbilical cord, ties it with a piece of worn cloth from the mother's dress, and buries it deep in the ground near the mother's hut. The elders believe that once planted, the umbilical cord never ceases to do its work; it continues to protect, sustain and provide energy to the person it had once nourished in the womb.

Tererai says, 'Both my grandmother and mother strongly believed that a child whose umbilical cord is buried in the ground will never forget their birthplace – their family and where they came from.'

Similarly, Tererai believed that her newly born dreams, now planted, would provide her energy, sustain her and never cease to remind her of what she wanted to achieve. And that her dreams would take root and flourish.

Eight long years of study by correspondence followed, driven by a burning desire to stop the cycle of poverty in her family, with Tererai sometimes waiting months for the arrival of the large brown envelope with her results. She calls it her eight years of failing and repeating. At the same time, she was working hard, raising her growing family, enduring regular and vicious beatings from her husband and saving every penny she could. Finally, after eight long years, she achieved the result she required for her university entrance.

In 1998, she was accepted as an undergraduate by Oklahoma State University. Tererai remembered her mother's wise words about the importance of giving back to the community. 'I knew I had a moral obligation, a sacred obligation, not only to educate myself, but also to educate my children and to come back with the gift of educating my own people. I had to make sure I took my children to America – especially the girls – so they didn't follow the same pathway [into early marriage] that I had.'

Tererai's husband eventually agreed that she could take the children to the United States – on condition that he went too. Through a combination of her own hard work and savings, and the help of those in her village, Tererai was able to purchase airline tickets for her family. Tererai's mother sold a cow and neighbours sold goats to help raise money. Even the poorest in the village gave what they could towards Tererai's dream. With US$4,000 in cash hidden in her clothes, Tererai finally set off for Oklahoma.

Her first impossible dream had come true, but the United States was no promised land. Tererai and her family had little money – the unfamiliar cold was relentless, they were constantly hungry, and their trailer house was cramped, rundown and without electricity. It was blisteringly hot in summer and freezing in winter.

Tererai often thought about quitting, but felt that doing so would let down other African women who would have loved the opportunity she had – and would mean breaking the sacred promises she had made to herself, symbolised by the buried dreams back in her village. So she struggled on, holding several jobs, taking every class she could, washing and scrubbing, enduring beatings from her husband and barely sleeping as she crammed so much into her day.

There were many times when Tererai was buoyed by the actions of a few good people. A university official, Dr Ron Beer, intervened on her behalf when she had difficulty with tuition fees and rallied the faculty and community behind her with donations and support.

'One day I noticed that when the children were brushing their teeth, their gums were bleeding. I realised that they were missing their fruits and vegetables. Back home, these were everywhere, but in America it was too expensive. I had to go to the university and beg them for help,' said Tererai.

An arrangement was made with a local supermarket manager for leftover fruit and vegetables to be placed in a box near the trash cans so Tererai could collect them. However, between university, holding down three jobs and taking care of five children, Tererai was often running late and had to fish the food out of the trash. 'Luckily, they clean their bins in America,' she said.

Things improved even more when Habitat for Humanity arranged better housing for the family and when Tererai's husband was deported back to Zimbabwe after she reported his abuse. Meanwhile, her dreams were coming to fruition. First, she earned her bachelor's degree, then her master's. And each time she returned home with one of those dreams accomplished, she'd check it off on that old, worn piece of paper that she'd buried so many years before.

News of her husband's ill health reached her: he'd become infected with AIDS. Some nailbiting months followed where Tererai waited to find out if he had infected her, but fate was on her side.

Through all these pressures, Tererai somehow found a way to excel at school, beginning a PhD at Western Michigan University with a dissertation on AIDS prevention programs for women and girls in Africa. She also, finally, found personal happiness too with her marriage to Mark Trent, a plant pathologist she had met at Oklahoma State.

Tererai is living proof of the power of dreaming and that the impossible *is* possible. As she shared with me...

'WHEN YOU WANT SOMETHING SO BADLY, KRISTINA, WHEN YOU HAVE A VISION TO CHANGE YOUR LIFE, WHEN YOU WRITE IT DOWN, IT BECOMES INGRAINED IN YOUR THOUGHTS. IT CAN BE MANIFESTED, BECAUSE YOUR MIND AND YOUR THOUGHTS AND YOUR FEELINGS BECOME FOCUSED ON THAT VISION.'

In 2009, almost twenty years after she first wrote down her dreams, the one-time cattle herder from Zimbabwe donned her academic robes and became Dr Tererai Trent, ticking off her dream of earning her PhD.

But there was one dream remaining – to take education back to her community. She began selling T-shirts printed with '*Tinogona* – it is achievable!' with the aim of funding her community education ideas, but with only twenty sold after a lot of effort, she began to lose hope. It was then she received a phone call that was to change her life.

Tererai's unlikely academic path has been featured in a book, *Half the Sky*,[1] and it caught the eye of producers at *The Oprah Winfrey Show*. An invitation to appear soon followed. Invited back a second time, Tererai was named by Oprah as her 'all-time favourite guest' and received a US$1.5 million donation to rebuild her childhood school in recognition of her persistence and never-say-never attitude.

Finally, Tererai was able to check off her final dream – to give back to her community. Now, as founder of Tererai Trent International, and through partnerships with Oprah Winfrey and Save the Children, Tererai's dream to provide universal access to education and empower rural communities continues to bear fruit. She has since built eleven schools in Zimbabwe that provide a strong start in life for many thousands of children. And this is only the beginning.

In 2017, Tererai published her book *The Awakened Woman* and she recently shared with me that her dream now is 'to sell ten million copies as a way to plant my dreams in women's hearts for a better world that un-silences women'. The proceeds from her book will be used to create employment centres for struggling rural women, helping them empower their children – particularly their girls – through education.

---

1   NICHOLAS D. KRISTOF AND SHERYL WUDANN, *HALF THE SKY: TURNING OPPRESSION INTO OPPORTUNITY FOR WOMEN WORLDWIDE* (NEW YORK: KNOPF, 2009)

Tinogona – it is achievable!

You can learn more about Tererai's story in her book, *The Awakened Woman: A Guide for Remembering & Reigniting Your Sacred Dreams* [2] (which won the 2018 NAACP Award for Outstanding Literary Work), in her children's book, *The Girl Who Buried Her Dreams in a Can*,[3] and at https://tererai.org. If her story has inspired you, maybe you could consider supporting her in some way to achieve her dream of bringing education to people who need it.

In Tererai's words, 'Many people have said to me "Tererai you must be an extraordinary individual" and I say no, I am just a girl from a tiny village in Zimbabwe, but I was given an opportunity to redesign the blueprint of my life.'

Let Tererai's amazing story inspire you to grasp the opportunity you have to redesign the blueprint of your life, to dream big for yourself and your loved ones. Take some time now while it's fresh in your mind to ponder on it – particularly on the power of giving yourself permission to dream – and, in the space below, or in your Dream Life Journal, write down anything you've learnt that you could apply in your own life.

You feel good helping others – migrane mandpus helped a lot of people!

I AM INCREDIBLY EXCITED TO BE DONATING US$1 FROM THE SALE OF EVERY BOOK TO THE TERERAI TRENT INTERNATIONAL FOUNDATION, TO HELP TERERAI BUILD ON THE GENEROUS SUPPORT FROM OPRAH, AND TO HELP ELEVATE HER DREAMS OF BRINGING UNIVERSAL ACCESS TO QUALITY EDUCATION FOR CHILDREN, REGARDLESS OF THEIR GENDER OR SOCIO-ECONOMIC BACKGROUNDS. AND I'M EVEN MORE EXCITED TO BE PARTNERING WITH TERERAI IN MANY OTHER WAYS TO SHARE OUR VERY SIMILAR MESSAGES AND EXPERIENCES OF THE POWER OF DREAMING WITH THE WORLD.

2   DR TERERAI TRENT, *THE AWAKENED WOMAN: A GUIDE FOR REMEMBERING & REIGNITING OUR SACRED DREAMS* (NEW YORK: ATRIA/ENLIVEN BOOKS, 2017)
3   DR TERERAI TRENT, *THE GIRL WHO BURIED HER DREAMS IN A CAN* (NEW YORK: PENGUIN PUTNAM INC, 2016)

YOU DON'T HAVE TO BE GREAT

TO START, BUT YOU HAVE TO

START TO BE GREAT.

- ZIG ZIGLAR -

CHAPTER THREE

START TODAY

YOUR DREAM LIFE STARTS HERE

There's no perfect day in the future to start creating your dream life. *Today* is the perfect day. It's so easy to put it off until tomorrow or Monday or the new year, but every day you put it off, your life is passing you by. Why wouldn't you start today?

Whenever I speak at events and meet people afterwards, I'm always asked: 'Where do I start?' And my answer is always the same. It doesn't matter where or how you start, the important thing is just to start. And that's exactly what you're doing right now. But before you continue on this journey, let me share a few thoughts...

I like to focus on dreaming and my personal development first thing in the morning – for an hour if I can. I'm less likely to be interrupted at this time and I find it sets me up for a great day.

I find it really useful to put the book I'm reading, my journal and a pen together in a storage box, so it's all in the one place. I love being organised and this helps me get into the flow quickly and get the day off to a smooth start. It's a small support system I put in place to help me. We'll come back to this idea of simple support systems later in the book when we move on to how to achieve your dreams...

You can choose whatever time suits you best and for how long you do it. But consider this: imagine if you spent an hour a day on dreaming and chasing your dreams. With seven days a week, that one hour out of the hustle and bustle of daily life becomes seven full hours a week. That's nearly an entire working day you've given yourself to work on your dreams, something that will bring you so much energy and inspiration.

OVER THE YEAR, THAT'S LIKE HAVING AN EXTRA DAY A WEEK TO WORK ON THE THINGS THAT TRULY MATTER TO YOU. THINGS THAT WILL MAKE A TRUE DIFFERENCE TO YOUR EXISTENCE.

Now an hour a day is not for everybody. You'll need to make your own decision on what time to invest and what pace to go at. There's no right or wrong. Just do what feels right for you.

Often people tell me they don't have an hour a day, and I always ask them if they can think of things they currently spend lots of time on that are less important to them and that they could reduce – for example, social media or watching television. I heard the other day that, on average, people check their smart devices 150 times a day! Even at just thirty seconds per check, that's more than an hour a day. Imagine the positive impact on your life if you spent just half of that time creating your dream life instead.

Don't get me wrong, I'm not against social media or watching television. Social media, in particular, serves a good purpose in so many ways, including bringing inspiration from all over the world to your fingertips. I just want you to stop and consciously think about where you spend your time and give yourself the opportunity to make a thoughtful decision on how else you could use it.

A good friend of mine told me how she downloaded an app that tracked the time she spent on various apps on her smartphone every day. She was astounded to find that she was spending three hours a day on average, most of which was spent on social media. Armed with that knowledge, she set herself boundaries around using her phone and scheduled time instead to chase her dreams – with great results.

When you actually write down how you spend your time over a day or a week, to the minute, you'll be amazed at how much time you can find to spend on things that will have a big positive impact on your life. My experience is that it's often the small tweaks that you make to your everyday routine that make the difference.

I've met many people who have had success with this exercise. In the words of one, '...it helped me find the one hour I needed to invest in this weekly. I call it "me time". I actually found more time than I thought was possible! Then I locked that time in my planner and shared it with my husband so he could see my "me time" too.'

So, today is the day and now is the time. I hope this excites you. There are so many amazing possibilities that lie ahead for you.

THE SECRET OF

GETTING AHEAD

IS GETTING

STARTED.

- SALLY BERGER -

EXERCISE

START NOW BY ANSWERING THESE QUESTIONS IN YOUR DREAM LIFE JOURNAL.

01 /

DECIDE WHAT DAY (AND TIME OF DAY) YOU'LL WORK THROUGH THIS BOOK AND THE EXERCISES.
I RECOMMEND THAT YOU MAKE IT AN HOUR A DAY - BECAUSE YOU'RE WORTH IT - BUT EVEN AN HOUR
ONCE A WEEK IS GREAT AND WILL HAVE YOU MOVING FORWARD. CHOOSE WHAT WORKS BEST FOR YOU.
THE KEY IS TO MAKE A DECISION YOU CAN COMMIT TO ON A REGULAR BASIS.

---

02 /

NOW HERE'S THE KEY - AND IT MIGHT BE ONE OF THE MOST IMPORTANT TASKS YOU'LL DO THIS YEAR.
OPEN YOUR DIARY AND WRITE IN APPOINTMENTS WITH YOURSELF ON ALL THE DAYS AND TIMES YOU'VE
DECIDED. DO YOUR BEST NOT TO MOVE THEM WHEN OTHER THINGS COME UP, AS THEY INVARIABLY
WILL. TREAT THIS TIME AS A VERY IMPORTANT MEETING WITH A VERY SPECIAL PERSON - YOU.

03/

MAKE A LIST OF THE THINGS YOU CURRENTLY SPEND TIME ON THAT YOU COULD POSSIBLY CUT BACK ON
TO FIND MORE TIME FOR WORKING ON YOU. WHAT ACTIVITIES COULD YOU REDUCE SO YOU CAN FOCUS
CLEARLY ON THIS IMPORTANT PRACTICE OF DREAMING AND CREATING YOUR DREAM LIFE?

04/

DECIDE IN ADVANCE *WHERE* YOU'LL DO YOUR DREAMING PRACTICE. SOMEWHERE YOU WON'T BE
INTERRUPTED. SOMEWHERE INSPIRING FOR YOU. KNOWING THIS AND LOCKING IT IN WILL HELP TAKE
AWAY A POTENTIAL BARRIER OR REASON TO PROCRASTINATE. HAVE EVERYTHING YOU NEED IN THE ONE
PLACE, SO YOU CAN SET UP, SETTLE IN AND GET PRODUCTIVE QUICKLY.

WHAT I FIND WORKS BEST FOR ME IS WHAT I CALL MY 'HOLY HOUR'. THIS IS WHEN I WORK ON MY
PERSONAL GROWTH, AT HOME AND EARLY IN THE MORNING BEFORE ANYONE ELSE IN THE FAMILY
WAKES SO I'M FREE OF INTERRUPTIONS. I MAKE MYSELF COMFORTABLE ON A SOFA, WITH A CANDLE
BURNING NEARBY AND WITH EVERYTHING I NEED WITHIN ARM'S REACH. BEAUTIFUL PENS, MY
JOURNALS, WATER, NOTEBOOK...

SO DECIDE ON A PLACE THAT WORKS FOR YOU, WHERE YOU WON'T BE INTERRUPTED. THIS COULD BE
YOUR BEDROOM OR ON YOUR SOFA. IT COULD BE IN A QUIET CORNER OF YOUR FAVOURITE CAFÉ OR
LYING IN YOUR LOCAL PARK. IT DOESN'T REALLY MATTER AS LONG AS IT'S A PLACE WHERE YOU ARE
COMFORTABLE AND INSPIRED TO WORK ON YOURSELF AND YOUR DREAMS.

EXERCISE

ACTIVITY	TIME SPENT ON IT EACH WEEK	TIME I CAN USE FROM THAT TO SPEND CREATING MY DREAM LIFE
E.G. SOCIAL MEDIA, TV	(GLOBALLY, PEOPLE SPEND AN AVERAGE OF 135 MINUTES PER DAY ON SOCIAL MEDIA)[4]	2 HOURS

4   STATISTA: THE STATISTICS PORTAL, 'DAILY TIME SPENT ON SOCIAL NETWORKING BY INTERNET USERS WORLDWIDE FROM 2012 TO 2017 (IN MINUTES)', SEPTEMBER 2017. HTTPS://WWW.STATISTA.COM/STATISTICS/433871/DAILY-SOCIAL-MEDIA-USAGE-WORLDWIDE/

FAMILY AND HOME

PERSONAL DEVELOPMENT AND ALL
THINGS TO IMPROVE MY LIFE

HEALTH AND WELLNESS

TRAVEL

SHARING INSPIRING AND EN
OTHERS

THE POWER OF PUTTING PEN TO PAPER

I take a notebook and pen with me everywhere. I'll jot down a great quote I come across, a new idea or add to my ever-growing list of dreams and goals.

I encourage you to carry a notebook and pen with you too so that you always have a way of capturing inspiration and no idea is lost. (Even if you think you'll remember something later, chances are you won't, given the distractions of modern life.) You can always revisit your notes later too, which is useful when you're reflecting on challenges or planning for a new year, month or week.

There's so much power in putting pen to paper. Research has actually shown that those who write down their dreams and goals on a regular basis are 42 per cent more likely to achieve them than those who don't.[5] And if you share those goals with someone in your life, the likelihood of you achieving those dreams and goals increases again – something we'll explore in chapter 16. So, just by those two simple actions, you can increase your chance of turning dreams into reality and move closer to your dream life. I think that's incredible. Such simple actions with such wonderful outcomes.

The reason why writing down your dreams can have such an amazing effect is because when you write them down, you acknowledge their importance and they become real. They go from being just a thought – a wish or hope – to a physical manifestation on paper.

Yes, you could get the words down faster by typing, but the pen is so much more powerful. Not only does writing encourage you to slow down – to think more deeply – it is also a truly personal act. And what could be more personal than your own dreams and goals?

Another benefit of taking dreams out of our hearts and heads and committing them to paper is that when we do that, we subconsciously (and consciously) start to take actions to make those dreams come true. It's almost like some sort of magic starts happening, although research[6] says that there is a sound scientific reason: the physical act of handwriting helps with memory, conceptual understanding and application. All things you'll need on your side as you pursue your dream life!

5   MATTHEWS, G. 2015. 'STUDY FOCUSES ON STRATEGIES FOR ACHIEVING GOALS, RESOLUTIONS.' IN *THE NINTH ANNUAL INTERNATIONAL CONFERENCE OF THE PSYCHOLOGY RESEARCH UNIT OF ATHENS INSTITUTE FOR EDUCATION AND RESEARCH* (ATINER), ATHENS, MAY 2015.

6   MUELLER, PAM A AND OPPENHEIMER, DANIEL. 'THE PEN IS MIGHTIER THAN THE KEYBOARD: ADVANTAGES OF LONGHAND OVER LAPTOP NOTE TAKING', PSYCHOLOGICAL SCIENCE 12, NO. 6 (2004), HTTP://JOURNALS.SAGEPUB.COM/DOI/ABS/10.1177/0956797614524581

START TODAY

1 THERE'S NO PERFECT DAY – THE
IMPORTANT THING IS JUST
TO START

2 COMMIT TO THE PROCESS
BY SETTING UP SYSTEMS TO
SUPPORT IT – AND HONOUR
YOURSELF AND YOUR DREAMS

3 IF YOU REALLY WANT
TO LIVE YOUR DREAM LIFE,
YOU'LL FIND OR MAKE
THE TIME TO WORK ON IT

CHAPTER FOUR

YOU'RE IN THE DRIVER'S SEAT

YOUR DREAM LIFE STARTS HERE

Before we get deeper into dreaming, I want you to know something important. Something that's essential to the work we'll do together in subsequent chapters.

YOU ARE IN CONTROL OF YOUR OWN LIFE.
IT'S YOU IN THE DRIVER'S SEAT.

Right now, you have everything you need to imagine the life you want to live and to transform yourself in whatever way you want. It's up to you to embrace your dreams and make them happen – to take control of your own personal growth and your experience of life. You don't need to wait for anyone or anything else to change or be different.

'YOU ARE ENTIRELY UP TO YOU.'
- ANON. -

Now does this idea excite and inspire you, or scare you? Take note of the feeling – maybe even scribble it in the space on the side of this paragraph. One day you'll be able to look back and remember exactly how you felt today.

You may already know and embrace this concept and maybe that's just how you live your life. If so, well done. I meet so many people who share with me that they can't see, for various reasons, how they can take control of their life. Or they understand the concept, but struggle to really embrace it at important moments.

After years of learning from experience and immersing myself in personal development material, I have absorbed so much. One of the most important lessons for me has been that – regardless of your education or circumstances – *you and only you can change your own life.*

As a teenager, I remember thinking that if my circumstances were different – if I had more knowledge, more experience, more money, if I had more education or lived in a big city – then my life would be better, more exciting and easier...

Looking back, it's clear that as a young girl I believed that external factors held more sway over my destiny than I did. I didn't stop to think about what *I* could do to make my life better. The 3am moment I talked about earlier was the turning point for me. Taking full control of my life for the first time was an indescribable, exciting feeling.

It's funny how many people think kikki.K was an overnight success story. If only. When I first started kikki.K, I quite literally lived on soup – it was cheap, healthy and I could save lots of time by cooking a big batch twice a week instead of cooking daily.

I worked breakfast and night shifts in hospitality so that I could spend my days working unpaid on my business dream. I borrowed $3,000 from my partner, Paul, to design and produce my first range of colour-matching folders, notebooks and storage boxes. Then I'd fill my car to overflowing with products (usually with the last box on my lap!) and drive to friends' homes to share my dream for kikki.K and offer my first products for sale. I maxed out every credit card I could get my hands on until I convinced Paul to sell his house so we could fund the launch of our very first kikki.K store – and yes, he's very grateful he did!

I did whatever I could to make it work because I knew it was up to me to do so. If I didn't take responsibility, then why would anyone else? This was my dream and I was in the driver's seat.

WHETHER YOU WANT TO...

+ START YOUR OWN BUSINESS
+ LAND A GREAT JOB OR GET PROMOTED
+ TAKE A SABBATICAL
+ CLIMB MOUNT EVEREST
+ MASTER A NEW LANGUAGE
+ BE THE BEST PARENT YOU CAN BE
+ BECOME A LEADER IN YOUR COMMUNITY

+ GRADUATE WITH A DEGREE
+ RAISE CHILDREN WHO WILL MAKE A DIFFERENCE IN THE WORLD
+ TAKE YOUR TALENT TO THE NEXT LEVEL
+ MAKE A LIVING FROM YOUR PASSION
+ WORK OUT WHAT'S NEXT FOR YOU AFTER YOUR CHILDREN HAVE LEFT HOME

...IT'S UP TO *YOU*

YOU HAVE BRAINS IN YOUR HEAD.

YOU HAVE FEET IN YOUR SHOES.

YOU CAN STEER YOURSELF ANY

DIRECTION YOU CHOOSE.

YOU'RE ON YOUR OWN. AND YOU

KNOW WHAT YOU KNOW.

AND YOU ARE THE ONE WHO'LL

DECIDE WHERE TO GO...

- DR SEUSS, *OH, THE PLACES YOU'LL GO!* -

EXERCISE

YOU HAVE EVERYTHING YOU NEED TO MAKE THE NECESSARY DECISIONS ALONG THE PATHWAY TO YOUR DREAM LIFE.

You can decide right now to change habits, to start something new or go after a goal. Or you can do the complete opposite. And it really doesn't matter what you choose, so long as you're happy with those decisions.

So my questions for you to contemplate and answer in your Dream Life Journal now, before you move onto the next chapter, are: →

'WHO YOU ARE TOMORROW BEGINS WITH WHAT YOU DO TODAY.'

- TIM FARGO -

EXERCISE

01 /

THINK OF SOMEONE YOU KNOW WHO STEERS THEIR JOURNEY THROUGH LIFE FROM THE DRIVER'S SEAT. WHAT DO YOU ADMIRE MOST ABOUT THEM? WHAT COULD YOU LEARN FROM THEM AND USE IN CREATING YOUR OWN DREAM LIFE?

02 /

WHAT ARE THREE KEY THINGS THAT HAVE HAPPENED IN THE LAST FEW YEARS THAT HAVE LED YOU TO WHERE YOU ARE TODAY?

03 /

FOR EACH, HOW MUCH WAS DRIVEN BY YOU? HOW MUCH WAS DRIVEN BY OTHER PEOPLE OR CIRCUMSTANCES BEYOND YOUR CONTROL? HOW DO YOU FEEL ABOUT THAT?

04 /

WHAT DO YOU NEED TO START DOING TO TAKE BETTER CONTROL OF YOUR LIFE? IN FACT, WHAT ARE THREE CHOICES THAT YOU CAN MAKE THIS WEEK THAT WILL GET YOU CLOSER TO YOUR DREAM LIFE NOW?

05 /

WHAT DO YOU NEED TO STOP DOING? WHAT IS NOT SERVING YOU WELL (FOR EXAMPLE, SAYING YES WHEN YOU REALLY WANT TO SAY NO)?

06 /

HOW STRONGLY DO YOU BELIEVE IN YOUR ABILITY TO TURN DREAMS INTO REALITY? (THIS IS A FUN QUESTION TO REVISIT IN A YEAR'S TIME, ONCE YOU'VE HAD TIME TO PRACTISE.)

07 /

KNOWING THAT HOW YOU FEEL EACH DAY IS ACTUALLY YOUR CHOICE, THINK ABOUT TO WHAT DEGREE THE WAY YOU LIVE YOUR LIFE NOW BRINGS YOU JOY. DO YOU WAKE UP EXCITED FOR THE DAY? HOW DO YOU WANT TO FEEL EACH DAY? WHAT THREE THINGS WILL YOU DO TO MAKE THAT FEELING A REALITY?

08 /

THINK ABOUT THE ANSWERS YOU'VE WRITTEN TO THE QUESTIONS ABOVE. DO ANY OF THEM PROMPT ANYTHING FOR YOU THAT YOU WANT TO ADD TO YOUR LIST OF 101 DREAMS? GO DO IT...

YOU'RE IN THE DRIVER'S SEAT

1 YOU ARE IN THE DRIVER'S SEAT OF YOUR OWN LIFE

2 YOU HAVE THE POWER TO CREATE CHANGE IF YOU WANT TO

3 IF YOU WANT TO CREATE CHANGE, YOU HAVE TO BELIEVE IN YOURSELF!

I AM NOT A PRODUCT OF MY

CIRCUMSTANCES.

I AM A PRODUCT OF

MY DECISIONS.

- STEPHEN COVEY -

'YOU ARE IN CONTROL OF THE CLICKER.'

ARIANNA HUFFINGTON

Arianna Huffington is such an inspiring woman. I first met her after reading her book *Thrive: The Third Metric to Redefining Success and Creating a Life of Well-Being, Wisdom, and Wonder,*[7] which I found so inspiring that I chased around after her to see if she wanted to collaborate to create a Thrive Collection for kikki.K so we could share the messages we both believe in more widely across the world. She did, and so that's what we did.

To the world, she's a Greek-American author, syndicated columnist and highly successful businesswoman, not to mention the co-founder and former Editor-in-Chief of *The Huffington Post* (which is now owned by AOL). To me, she's a friend and sometimes mentor – no fuss, straight shooter – and I cherish the times we get to catch up when our busy paths cross.

In 2009, Arianna was ranked twelfth in *Forbes* first-ever list of the 'Most Influential Women in Media'. In 2014, she was listed by *Forbes* as the fifty-second 'Most Powerful Woman in the World'. Both achievements are a far cry from her humble childhood beginnings.

There is so much inspiration to be drawn from Arianna's life – and I urge you to read her books and research her story for yourself – but I learnt two key things from her story. Simple things, but so very valuable, and I want to focus you on them both to help guide your dreaming journey. First, that looking at the world with a sense of wonder, no matter what life throws at you, is a brilliant attitude to cultivate. Second, that we are all in the drivers' seats of our own lives.

In her book *Thrive*, Arianna explains how one of the gifts her mother passed on to her was her sense of curiosity and wonder.

'Countless things in our daily lives can awaken the almost constant state of wonder we knew as children,' says Arianna, '...but sometimes to see them we must look through a different set of eyes.'

---

7   ARIANNA HUFFINGTON, *THE THIRD METRIC TO REDEFINING SUCCESS AND CREATING A LIFE OF WELL-BEING, WISDOM, AND WONDER* (NEW YORK: HARMONY BOOKS, 2014)

Taking time out to consciously dream – to open your heart and practise dreaming in an unconstrained way – is one highly valuable way for you to look at the world through a different set of eyes. Take inspiration from Arianna and bring that into your life.

Whenever Arianna was upset or would complain about something, her mother would say, 'Just change the channel. You are in control of the clicker. Don't replay the bad, scary movie.' This sound advice has served Arianna well – she's someone clearly in the driver's seat of her own life, who chooses to focus on solutions rather than complaining about problems, which has helped her inspire millions through her books, businesses and media appearances.

Another gem from Arianna's story that I love is her view that it's not 'What do I want to do?', it's 'What kind of life do I want to live?' A woman truly after my own heart, Arianna is living proof that it's possible, if you want, to dream up and create a dream life for you and your loved ones.

Let Arianna's story inspire you to take control of your life. Take some time now while it's fresh in your mind to think about it and, in the space below, or in your Dream Life Journal, write down anything you've learnt that you could apply in your own life.

THE ONLY THING THAT WILL

STOP YOU FROM FULFILLING

YOUR DREAMS IS YOU.

- TOM BRADLEY -

CHAPTER FIVE

WHO ARE YOU AND WHERE ARE YOU AT RIGHT NOW?

YOUR DREAM LIFE STARTS HERE

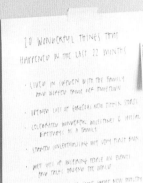

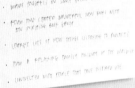

10 WONDERFUL THINGS THAT
HAPPENED IN THE LAST 22 MONTHS

· LIVED IN SWEDEN WITH THE FAMILY
  AND VISITED MANY MY HOMETOWN

· OPENED LOTS OF GORGEOUS NEW ZIPPER STORES

· CELEBRATED WONDERFUL MILESTONES & SPECIAL
  BIRTHDAYS AS A FAMILY

· GREATLY UNDERSTANDING MY OWN TRUST BANK

· MET LOTS OF INSPIRING PEOPLE AT EVENTS
  AND TALKS AROUND THE WORLD

· MADE PROGRESS ON SOME GREAT NEW BUILDING IDEALS

· READ AND STARTED WONDERFUL NEW BOOKS WITH
  MY INSPIRING BOOK GROUP

· LEARNT LOTS OF NEW THINGS WITHIN MY PASSIONS

· TOOK A RELAXING FAMILY HOLIDAY IN MY HOMETOWN

· CONNECTED WITH PEOPLE THAT TRULY INSPIRED ME

Being an avid reader of everything I can lay my hands on in the personal development space, I'm constantly inspired to improve my life. I write notes and ideas in my journal every day and, over the years, I've learnt that you need to know where you are before you can decide where you want to go. And how you will get there.

Think about your current circumstances. Where are you at right now? And what brought you to this place? To go from dreaming to doing, you need knowledge of yourself and an awareness of the journey you've already taken, including decisions you have made along the way that have brought you to where you are today.

When I look back over my life, I can identify a number of important moments when I've made big decisions or experienced events that changed the course of my life and shaped the person I am today.

Deciding to move to Melbourne from Sweden and start a new life in a new country was one of those moments. Deciding to start my own business and launch kikki.K was another. Others include supporting my younger brother, Hans, through serious illness, deciding to become a mother and, just recently, taking the decision to live in Sweden for a year with our two young children, which had long been a family dream. Being asked to speak publicly and choosing to do that was a pivotal moment too – it was one thing I really feared – and while I still don't love it, I do love sharing my experiences with others and seeing how that inspires people.

When I think about decisive moments like these, I remember feeling both terrified and excited at the same time. Oddly enough, I've grown to *love* that feeling. It's when I know I'm doing something that matters, something that will push me and help me grow. That feeling is a great sign that you're moving out of your comfort zone and towards your dream life.

Looking back over your own life, you'll recognise that you've achieved so much already and it's those moments that can inspire you to push even further and dream even bigger. Our life stories make us who we are – and they influence our view of the future. Our dreams.

One of my favourite quotes is by Aristotle:

'KNOWING YOURSELF IS THE BEGINNING OF ALL WISDOM.'

I love these words. The more self-awareness you have and the more you know yourself, the more you're able to understand why you make certain decisions, why you form certain habits and, importantly, what makes you feel your best.

If you know these things, you can learn what you need to make time for and how to live your best life. Self-awareness is about being honest with yourself and looking at your life without judgement. It's about understanding what your strengths and weaknesses are at any given point in your life, what influences your decisions and whether your attitude and mindset is serving you or holding you back. It's also about understanding the choices you make, without feeling guilty or ashamed if you fall short of your ideal.

You might find the process of looking deep into yourself a little confronting and challenging. That's a good thing. When you're out of your comfort zone, you know you're growing personally. Stick with me here and trust me that it's worth doing this well.

A few years ago, after a session reflecting on where I was at, I had been wrestling with why it was so difficult to get out of bed early in the mornings. I love mornings, but I'd slipped into a pattern of not sleeping well, which made it hard to rise and shine when I wanted to. Through that process of self-reflection, I realised that the couple of glasses of wine I was having with dinner during the week was probably affecting my ability to sleep well, which was making it hard for me to get up and do the exercise and other things I wanted to do in the early morning.

That led me to challenge myself to give up alcohol and sugar for three months to see if I could sleep better. I *did* sleep better. And it did help me get up earlier and exercise, which in turn helped me feel more energetic and creative, and get more done. The experience taught me some good lessons about balancing my life.

ACCEPT YOURSELF AS YOU ARE, WHILE ALWAYS STRIVING TO BE BETTER AND IMAGINING THE FUTURE YOU WANT TO CREATE.

Something I do at the end of every year is to answer the list of questions at the end of this chapter. This helps me understand who I am and where I'm at, at this particular point in time (remembering that we're all always evolving). It's a great place to start before deciding where I want to go in the next twelve months and what dreams I want to chase.

I have a dream that I never want to live the same year twice. I always want to add something different to the new year ahead. This makes me carefully look through my list of dreams each year and intentionally choose to focus on adding something new to my life. I love thinking and pondering what this can be as I reflect on where I am in life at my annual check-in.

I usually do this in November or December when I'm starting to set goals and plan for the new year, but you can do it whenever you choose. I always have my previous journals and diary handy, to glance through and remind myself just how much I managed to squeeze in over the preceding year. It's a beautiful, feel-good exercise and something I always anticipate eagerly.

EXERCISE

Work through these questions for yourself now. Then have fun filling out the charts to create a visual representation too. Use the space in your Dream Life Journal to jot down your answers and reflect on them afterwards. Keep your answers somewhere safe so that you can revisit them next year or whenever you need.

01 /

REFLECT AND WRITE DOWN YOUR ANSWERS TO:

+ TEN WONDERFUL THINGS THAT HAPPENED IN THE LAST TWELVE MONTHS
+ FIVE THINGS I'M MOST PROUD OF FROM THE LAST TWELVE MONTHS
+ FIVE LESSONS I LEARNT IN THE LAST TWELVE MONTHS
+ FIVE THINGS I WANT TO DO LESS OF, OR NOT AT ALL, IN THE NEXT TWELVE MONTHS
+ FIVE THINGS I WANT TO DO MORE OF IN THE NEXT TWELVE MONTHS
+ FIVE THINGS I'M GRATEFUL FOR IN THE LAST TWELVE MONTHS
+ FIVE THINGS I DID THAT TOOK ME CLOSER TO LIVING MY DREAM LIFE IN THE LAST TWELVE MONTHS
+ FIVE THINGS I WANT TO DO TO IMPROVE MY LIFE
+ FIVE GREAT DECISIONS I MADE IN THE LAST TWELVE MONTHS
+ IF I COULD LIVE THE LAST TWELVE MONTHS AGAIN, WHAT WOULD I CHANGE AND WHY?

---

02 /

REFLECT AT A HIGH LEVEL ON THE FOLLOWING AREAS OF YOUR LIFE AND GIVE YOURSELF A RATING OUT OF TEN FOR EACH (WITH 10 BEING 'I'M COMPLETELY SATISFIED WITH MY LIFE IN THIS AREA' AND 1 BEING 'I'M COMPLETELY UNSATISFIED WITH MY LIFE IN THIS AREA'). COLOUR IN THE BAR CHART TO GIVE YOURSELF A CLEAR VISUAL INDICATION OF WHERE YOU ARE AT RIGHT NOW.

+ CAREER AND FINANCES
+ EDUCATION AND LEARNING
+ HEALTH, WELLNESS AND FITNESS
+ FAMILY AND RELATIONSHIPS
+ HOME
+ SPIRITUALITY AND/OR SENSE OF PURPOSE
+ TRAVEL AND EXPERIENCES
+ HOBBIES/FUN
+ COMMUNITY AND ENVIRONMENT

EXERCISE

CAREER AND FINANCES

1	2	3	4	5	6	7	8	9	10

EDUCATION AND LEARNING

1	2	3	4	5	6	7	8	9	10

HEALTH, WELLNESS AND FITNESS

1	2	3	4	5	6	7	8	9	10

FAMILY AND RELATIONSHIPS

1	2	3	4	5	6	7	8	9	10

HOME

1	2	3	4	5	6	7	8	9	10

SPIRITUALITY AND SENSE OF PURPOSE

1	2	3	4	5	6	7	8	9	10

TRAVEL AND EXPERIENCES

1	2	3	4	5	6	7	8	9	10

HOBBIES/FUN

1	2	3	4	5	6	7	8	9	10

COMMUNITY AND ENVIRONMENT

1	2	3	4	5	6	7	8	9	10

EXERCISE

03 /

NOW, ON THE SAME CHART, USE A DIFFERENT COLOUR TO INDICATE WHERE YOU WOULD LIKE TO BE FOR EACH CATEGORY. YOU MAY SET THE BAR HIGHER, LOWER OR EVEN LEAVE IT EXACTLY AS IT IS TODAY. REMEMBER, THIS IS JUST A VERY HIGH-LEVEL EXERCISE TO GET YOU THINKING.

I'M A BIG BELIEVER IN THE FACT THAT YOU CAN DO ANYTHING – JUST NOT EVERYTHING AT THE SAME TIME. IN MY OWN LIFE, I CUT BACK ON PUBLIC SPEAKING AND WORK AFTER THE BIRTH OF MY CHILDREN, KNOWING THAT I REALLY WANTED TO FOCUS MORE ON FAMILY, ONE OF MY CORE VALUES.

MAYBE THIS YEAR YOU WILL CHOOSE TO FOCUS ON JUST ONE OR TWO KEY AREAS, AND THAT'S FINE. WHAT'S MOST IMPORTANT IS GETTING A CLEAR IDEA OF WHERE YOU WANT TO BE. AND THIS IS THE EXCITING PART!

---

04 /

REFLECT ON WHAT THIS CHART IS TELLING YOU. DOES IT REVEAL ANYTHING ABOUT WHAT YOUR PRIORITIES SHOULD BE FOR THE NEXT TWELVE MONTHS? MAKE A NOTE, AND I ENCOURAGE YOU TO REFLECT AND COMPLETE THIS EXERCISE AGAIN IN TWELVE MONTHS. PUT A REMINDER IN YOUR DIARY.

---

05 /

REFLECT ON WHETHER ANYTHING FROM THIS EXERCISE HAS TRIGGERED ANY DREAMS TO BE ADDED TO YOUR 101 DREAMS LIST, AND THEN GO ADD THEM.

ONLY WHEN WE ARE BRAVE

ENOUGH TO EXPLORE OUR

DARKNESS WILL WE DISCOVER

THE INFINITE POWER

OF OUR LIGHT.

- BRENÉ BROWN -

WHO ARE YOU AND WHERE ARE YOU AT RIGHT NOW

1
THE MORE SELF-AWARE
YOU ARE, THE BETTER
YOU CAN ADAPT
AND GROW

2
THE MORE YOU CAN ADAPT
AND GROW, THE BETTER YOU
CAN LIVE YOUR DREAM LIFE

3
YOU CAN GROW YOUR
SELF-AWARENESS THROUGH
REFLECTION, JOURNALLING
AND LEARNING

'I THOUGHT AGAIN OF THE LITTLE FROG IN THE WELL...'

LI CUNXIN

I will never forget having the honour of hearing Li Cunxin tell his life story firsthand. How he survived a childhood of bitter poverty and, inspired by his dreams, became one of the world's best male ballet dancers. Not an eye in the room was dry and we all left that day incredibly inspired and grateful for the many learnings we had made about the power of dreams ... and how to make them come true.

I subsequently read his autobiography, *Mao's Last Dancer*,[8] watched the feature film adapted from this book when it came out in 2009 and after stumbling upon his children's book, *The Peasant Prince*,[9] have read that many times to my children. They love it and we've spent many hours talking about the inspiration we all draw from his story. You really must read his books and watch the movie.

Li grew up in bitter poverty near the city of Qingdao, in Shandong province in north-east China. Born in 1961, the sixth of seven brothers, into a poor rural family, his childhood coincided with a period in China's history when food was scarce for millions. Li recalls: 'When we all sat down to eat, we would stare longingly at what little food there was. Every night our mother would pray that none of her sons would die from starvation. I was always hungry.'

One of the most compelling elements of his life story for me was his very clear memory of a story that his father told him many times as a child, his fascination with that story and the way that story inspired him to dream. In a way, it's a little like the theme we explored in chapter 2 of how you can be inspired by the dreams and stories of others.

The story was about a frog that lived at the bottom of a deep, dark well from which there was no chance of escape to the bigger, better world above. It was clear his father was referencing the poor circumstances in which the family lived – stuck in poverty – and, like the little frog, their slim chance of escaping.

But the way his father told the story gave Li hope and fuelled his childhood dreams to one day help his family escape the poverty they were all trapped in.

---

8   LI CUNXIN, *MAO'S LAST DANCER* (MELBOURNE: PENGUIN VIKING, 2003)

9   LI CUNXIN, *THE PEASANT PRINCE* (MELBOURNE: PENGUIN VIKING, 2007)

Li's father recounted in his story that despite the frog's father telling the little frog 'there is no way you can get out of here ... I've tried all my life ... forget the world above', the little frog still 'spent his life trying to escape the cold, dark well'. The tale gave Li hope, helped him cope with monumental challenges, and fuelled his dream to escape poverty and to help his family.

'I thought about that poor frog in the well many times,' says Li. And he recalls the story affecting him so strongly as a young child that he would attach three dreams to his kite and fly them as 'messages to the gods'. 'My first wish was for my mother's happiness and long life. My second wish was for my father's happiness and long life. My third wish was to get out of the deep dark well. I dreamed about all the beautiful things in life that were not mine. Food for my family. I begged the gods to get me out of the well so I could help my family.'

Similar to Dr Tererai Trent's story, Li was linking his dreams to the betterment of others – his family – and he was instinctively giving his dreams symbolic importance, bringing them to life by tying them to his kite and flying them up into the sky.

Things took a turn when Li was eleven. He recalls: 'One very cold day, four strange officials came into our classroom. They wanted to take some children to study something called ballet. Only one girl was chosen from my class. Then, just as they were about to leave, Teacher Song suddenly pointed at me. "What about that one?" she said. "Okay, he can come too," was the answer.' It was a moment that, by the thinnest thread of a chance, changed the course of his life.

He joined a group of about ten other children from other classes that day who were all measured and tested. 'My legs were lifted high, my body was stretched,' he remembers. 'Other children cried out in pain, but I did not. I thought again of the little frog in the well. Perhaps if I could pass this test I could help my family live a better life.' Li's dream had been the driving force for him to summon his courage and find a way to turn this stroke of luck into the opportunity of a lifetime.

For many weeks he waited. Then came the exciting news! Li Cunxin, a poor peasant boy, had been chosen from millions of children in the whole of China. He was to leave home and become a dancer. He remembers his mother saying to him, 'My dear son, this is your one chance to escape this cruel world. You have your secret dreams. Follow them! Make them come true!' And he did.

Li struggled at first with ballet and a harsh regime that included a gruelling sixteen hours a day of training, starting each morning at 5:30am. He also recalls being desperately sad at being separated from his beloved family at such a young age, and crying himself to sleep most nights.

However, through great courage, determination and hard work – driven by dreams of helping his family one day and with the guidance of a teacher named Xiao – by the end of the seven-year training he had become a very good dancer. One of China's best.

He was one of the first students from the Beijing Dance Academy to go to the United States on a scholarship to dance with the Houston Ballet in 1979, and famously created headlines when he defected to the West. This resulted in his Chinese citizenship being revoked. As a result, he was cut off from his beloved family for nine years, before eventually being able to fulfil his dream of helping them out of poverty. He remembers with excitement when he was finally allowed back into China in June 1988, returning home with five suitcases full of gifts and buying two much-needed refrigerators for his family.

Li danced with the Houston Ballet for sixteen years, achieving the rank of Principal in 1982. He won many awards and accolades, including two silver medals and one bronze medal at three international ballet competitions and two highly prestigious Princess Grace Awards, in the process becoming one of the world's best male ballet dancers.

There is so much more to his remarkable story, a story that demonstrates that it's possible to rise from even the most awful circumstances if you have a dream, if it's strong enough, if you believe in it and if you work hard. Despite enormous obstacles, Li's dreams pulled him forwards and opened him up to possibility, preparing him for those moments in his life when opportunities presented themselves.

Li fell in love with Australian dancer, Mary McKendry, a Principal Dancer with the Houston Ballet, and eventually made his way to settle and start a family in Melbourne, Australia. He turned his hand to finance after his dancing career, building a successful and lucrative career as a stockbroker before giving it up to again follow his passion for the art form of ballet. He is now the Artistic Director of Queensland Ballet – a vibrant, creative and world-class company – where his purpose has turned to helping others make their dreams come true through ballet. His dreams are truly tied to the dreams of others.

Let Li's amazing story inspire you to dream big for yourself and your loved ones. Take some time now while it's fresh in your mind to ponder on it and write down anything you've learnt that you could apply in your own life over the page or in your Dream Life Journal.

A DREAM WITHOUT A PLAN

IS JUST A WISH.

- KATHERINE PATERSON -

DON'T ASK WHAT THE WORLD

NEEDS. ASK WHAT MAKES YOU

COME ALIVE, AND GO DO IT.

BECAUSE WHAT THE WORLD

NEEDS IS PEOPLE WHO HAVE

COME ALIVE.

- HOWARD THURMAN -

6

DISCOVER AND FOLLOW YOUR PASSIONS

YOUR DREAM LIFE STARTS HERE

Imagine what it would be like to spend most of your time doing things you don't like, in an environment you don't like, surrounded by people you don't like. Not much fun?

In my experience, the answer to avoiding this trap has been to follow my passions – to spend as much time as possible doing things that I love and that make me feel truly alive. For me, because I realised that in life we usually need to spend a lot of time working, I decided that combining work and my passions made sense.

When your work involves something you care deeply about, then you have the chance to live and breathe your passion. For example, I started doing Arianna's online *Thrive* course out of personal interest, but this soon blurred into work as I loved it so much that we ended up doing a collaboration with her. Lots of my big ideas come when I'm doing a course, reading or simply out walking. It's then I feel as if my life, work and purpose go hand in hand. It simply doesn't feel like I'm working – more like I'm living my purpose. You deserve to have that feeling too.

That does not mean that life then becomes a breeze. Even when you follow your passions, there are ups and downs, and things you need to do that are less enjoyable than others. But if you are pursuing a dream you are passionate about, you will never be too far away from things that you really value and love. Understanding and being deep in financials helps me run my business better, so I can see its inherent value, even though it's certainly not as close to my heart as, say, design.

So ... when people ask me, as they often do, 'What is the number one thing to know about starting a business?', I always answer: 'Find something you're passionate about.'

I give the same answer when people tell me they don't enjoy their jobs. And this doesn't just apply to starting a business or to finding a career you love – I believe it applies to *anything* you want to do in life. Life is short and you deserve to spend as much of your precious time doing things you are passionate about, that give you a sense of meaning and joy, and which bring you into regular contact with like-minded people. Seriously, you deserve this.

The wonderful news is that you have a choice. You are in the driver's seat. You can choose to find and follow passions and you can also choose to move away from things you don't love – things that sap your spirit rather than giving you energy and joy. That's worth reflecting on.

Many people tell me it's not so easy finding things to feel passionate about. So, in this chapter, we're going to do some thinking and exercises to explore and help get you closer to finding out what your true passions are. I do these exercises every year and recommend you do them yearly too. Over time, we all grow and change, as do our priorities and interests, so it's worth checking in annually on this.

When I was searching for my 'thing' – my passion – kikki.K wasn't the first option I explored. When I was still at school, and trying to figure out what I wanted to do when I finished, for some reason optometry came to mind. Then I discovered that it's a very hard course to get into in Sweden, so I'd have to work very hard to get the necessary marks.

That's when I decided it might first be a good idea to see what being an optometrist was really like. I contacted the local optometrist in my hometown of Falkenberg, Sweden, and asked if I could work for free every Thursday afternoon in return for the opportunity to learn more about optometry as a career.

A couple of months were enough for me to know that glasses and eyes were *not* my destiny. I was very grateful that I found out so quickly, rather than after years of study. So I continued my search, but without knowing what I know today about dreaming – and am sharing here with you – I was still feeling my way.

IF ONLY ALL SCHOOLS TAUGHT CHILDREN HOW TO FIND THEIR PASSIONS!

When I moved to Melbourne at twenty-two, I still had no idea what to do with my life. One of the first things I thought of after my 3am List experience was that I was passionate about travel. So perhaps a career in travel? I'd always loved to travel, so it seemed an obvious choice.

Off I went and I asked everyone I met if they knew anyone who worked in travel. I met as many people in the industry as I could, peppering them with questions about what they did, what they liked about it, what they didn't like, how they got into it, and so on.

This helped me understand the industry a bit better and gave me the confidence to literally knock on the door of an award-winning travel agent and explain that I was interested in a career in travel. Again, I offered to work for free to gain experience. I also suggested – a little bit cheekily – that they might give me a job one day if they decided I could add value to their business.

After two weeks of happily working for nothing in exchange for the opportunity and experience, they offered me a paid role! I stayed there for more than a year – and learnt lots – but the most important thing I learnt was that booking other people's travel didn't make me excited to drive to work on a Monday morning. I'd have to continue my search. It was a really valuable learning experience.

It wasn't long after, when I was almost boiling with frustration about not knowing what I wanted to do and struggling to find beautiful stationery products to set up my home office, that I finally landed on the idea of kikki.K. Combining my love of design with my love of Sweden and my deep passion for learning, I began building a brand and a business that I absolutely love. Through all the ups and downs, the energy I get from it is amazing. I believe everyone deserves to find their passion, whether it becomes a career or not, and embrace it as part of a life they love.

IF YOU LOVE WHAT YOU DO, YOU'VE ALREADY WON HALF THE BATTLE. AND IF YOU DON'T LOVE WHAT YOU DO, NOW'S THE TIME TO START EXPLORING.

Are you in a similar situation to the one I was in? Are you unsure about what you want to do or if your planned career or direction in life is actually for you?

Above all, I encourage you to work for free or volunteer to get a true hands-on insight into whatever you think might be your thing. My experience is that nothing beats that. Now some people may see difficulties, like finding the time, finding a suitable organisation or finding someone to give you a chance. If your dream is strong enough, you will find a way.

I also encourage you to ask around and talk to people already in the area that interests you, to do a short course in that area and read and research as much as you can.

Do you know someone who is already doing what you want to do? Or do you know of someone who's working in your dream role? If you're starting a business, do you know someone who has done something similar before, even if it's in a different area?

Ask people you admire how they got to where they are and if they can offer advice or support in any way. Seek out people who are doing what you want to do and offer to buy them lunch so you can ask your questions. Be specific. Many people have limited time so make sure you go with a list of prepared questions, take note of any learnings in a notebook, and be sure to show that you value and respect their time.

This was one of the most helpful actions I took when I was first starting kikki.K. I contacted people I admired, who had done what I wanted to do – set up a successful retail business – and asked to meet them for coffee. I asked specific questions: How did they get started? What were the challenges? What did they love about what they did? What would they do differently?

I literally filled my journal with notes and they almost always pointed me to other people who might be able to help. Many of these people became great supporters over the years. I always followed up with a handwritten thank-you card and an offer to help them in the future if the opportunity arose. Often people went well out of their way to help me. I believe this had a lot to do with the respect I showed for their time and an innate human instinct to help others who are trying to help themselves improve. You have to always think and act win-win – give something back to people who help you.

If you're interested in talking to a public figure or well-known person who may be hard to meet, then what can you read or learn about them elsewhere? So much of what I've learnt in business has been from books, seminars and courses. There is so much content and knowledge available to us today at the click of a button.

I'M CONVINCED THAT THE ONLY

THING THAT KEPT ME GOING WAS

THAT I LOVED WHAT I DID. YOU'VE

GOT TO FIND WHAT YOU LOVE ...

AND LOVE WHAT YOU DO.

– STEVE JOBS –
2005 STANFORD COMMENCEMENT ADDRESS

EXERCISE

In your Dream Life Journal (or using the list on the opposite page), write down your passions. To help you:

01 /

THERE'S A LOT YOU CAN DO TO EXPLORE AND DISCOVER YOUR PASSIONS. I'VE PUT TOGETHER A LIST OF QUESTIONS I LOVE TO ASK TO HELP GET YOU STARTED. DON'T BE AFRAID TO TRY NEW THINGS AND EXPLORE NEW PASSIONS TOO. IT'S SO VALUABLE TO CREATE A LIST (OR LISTS) OF THINGS YOU'RE PASSIONATE ABOUT. YOU CAN ADD TO IT, REVIEW IT AND EDIT IT OVER TIME. MAKE A START NOW – AND WE'LL RETURN TO THIS LIST LATER TO HELP YOU DESIGN A LIFE YOU LOVE.

+ WHAT DO YOU LOVE TO DO?
+ WHAT DO YOU FIND YOURSELF DOING IN YOUR SPARE TIME?
+ WHAT DO YOU ALWAYS MAKE TIME FOR?
+ WHAT ARE YOU REALLY GOOD AT? WHAT ARE YOUR SKILLS AND STRENGTHS? WHAT'S YOUR MAGIC?
+ WHAT DO YOU CARE DEEPLY ABOUT?
+ THINK ABOUT TIMES WHEN YOU COMPLETELY LOST TRACK OF TIME – JUST ENJOYING WHAT YOU WERE DOING AND TOTALLY IN THE FLOW. WHAT WAS IT YOU WERE DOING? IS THERE SOMETHING IN THAT THAT COULD INDICATE A PASSION FOR YOU TO FOLLOW?

IF, WHEN ANSWERING THE QUESTIONS ABOVE, YOU THINK 'I GET LOST ON SOCIAL MEDIA FOR HOURS' – AND THAT HAPPENS TO MANY – THINK ABOUT WHAT IT IS THAT'S CAPTURING YOUR INTEREST. MAYBE IT'S YOUR INTEREST IN FOOD, FASHION OR HEALTH THAT MAKES YOU FIND IT COMPELLING? MAYBE IT'S THE WAY PEOPLE YOU FOLLOW ARE TRAVELLING, ARE FIT AND HEALTHY, OR ARE MAKING A DIFFERENCE IN THEIR WORLD? PONDER WHAT THIS MEANS FOR YOU AND IF THOSE THINGS SHOW WHAT YOU ARE PASSIONATE ABOUT.

I FIND THAT HAVING SOMEONE TO DISCUSS THESE EXERCISES WITH IS REALLY HELPFUL. TALKING THROUGH MY THOUGHTS OUT LOUD WITH SOMEONE I RESPECT AND TRUST OFTEN ADDS VALUE, HELPING MAKE IT CLEARER FOR ME. I RECOMMEND YOU DO THAT TOO.

02 /

NOW LOOK BACK OVER THIS LIST. HOW COULD YOU COMBINE YOUR PASSIONS WITH YOUR STRENGTHS TO CREATE NEW DREAMS – TO BUILD A FULFILLING NEW CAREER OR EXPLORE AN EXCITING NEW HOBBY OR SIDE PROJECT? ADD ANY NEW DREAMS THAT SURFACE OUT OF THIS EXERCISE TO YOUR 101 DREAMS LIST.

01	_____	26	_____
02	_____	27	_____
03	_____	28	_____
04	_____	29	_____
05	_____	30	_____
06	_____	31	_____
07	_____	32	_____
08	_____	33	_____
09	_____	34	_____
10	_____	35	_____
11	_____	36	_____
12	_____	37	_____
13	_____	38	_____
14	_____	39	_____
15	_____	40	_____
16	_____	41	_____
17	_____	42	_____
18	_____	43	_____
19	_____	44	_____
20	_____	45	_____
21	_____	46	_____
22	_____	47	_____
23	_____	48	_____
24	_____	49	_____
25	_____	50	_____

DISCOVER AND FOLLOW YOUR PASSIONS

1 IF YOU LOVE WHAT YOU DO, YOU'VE ALREADY WON HALF THE BATTLE. AND IF YOU DON'T LOVE WHAT YOU DO, NOW'S THE TIME TO START EXPLORING

2 EMBRACING YOUR PASSIONS GIVES YOUR LIFE MEANING AND JOY

3 GET CREATIVE TO DISCOVER YOUR PASSIONS – WORK FOR FREE, ASK PEOPLE IN SIMILAR SITUATIONS, TAKE COURSES, LEARN AND STUDY

'TRY SOMETHING NEW – YOU CAN DO IT!'

LISA LEMKE

I love my family, I love my home, I love writing and I love food. So I think that's one of the reasons why Lisa Lemke's pursuit of her dream life really inspires me. Somehow she's managed to combine all of this, and along the way she's created her dream life. Follow your passions!

I first met Lisa when I visited her beautiful backyard restaurant, Prostens Pizza, just out of my hometown of Falkenberg, on the west coast of Sweden. It was genuinely one of the best food experiences of my life. We'd ridden our bikes five kilometres through the lush forest to get there, then sat in her country garden for pre-dinner drinks with friends, surrounded by flowers, children and happy people as the sun slowly set on a balmy summer evening... The food was simple and amazing, and Lisa's hospitality was warm and genuine as she wandered around making people feel welcome. I asked her what her story was and, as you'll read below, you'll see how easy it was to be drawn to and inspired by the lovely Lisa, who is now a great friend.

Today, Lisa's face is instantly recognised by Swedish television viewers and thousands of online followers around the world. It's a long way from her childhood in rural Sweden where she dreamed of being a dairy farmer and filled notebook after notebook with potential names for all her future cows.

Later on, after a visit to the local newspaper, Lisa decided that perhaps writing was more to her taste, so she swapped her dream career from dairy farming to journalism.

'Crash, boom, bang – I fell totally in love with the world of words. Imagine writing for a living, every day and every year!' says Lisa.

Lisa's story is an important reminder that we all change and evolve over time, as do our dreams, and that embracing change and reimagining our dreams can lead us to shape a life that's just right for us.

Throughout her school years, Lisa talked herself into internships at newspapers and radio stations, and was blown away when she was offered a proper paying job at the local newspaper during the summer holidays. 'I was the proudest seventeen-year-old on earth!' she says.

On graduating high school, Lisa went on to study journalism at university, but the more she studied and the more she kept working part-time at the paper, the more strongly she felt that maybe – just perhaps – her dream career had changed. 'One big clue was that my interviews kept getting side-tracked into conversations about cinnamon rolls and barbecue techniques,' she says.

It was while she was studying in Edinburgh that the thunderbolt struck. 'I realised that I didn't have to choose between writing and my passion for food. I could simply write about food.'

Lisa took the plunge and set herself up as a freelance food writer. It took time, but slowly the pile of rejection emails turned to requests for her work. Her first cookbook followed and then she transferred her talents to television as host of the popular Swedish morning show, *My Kitchen*.

Lisa credits her success not only to hard work, but also to never (okay, almost never) being afraid of saying yes – even when she's not 100 per cent sure that she knows what to do and is scared to death. Unsurprisingly, one of her favourite sayings is: 'I have never tried that before, so I think I should definitely be able to do that' from the classic children's book, *Pippi Longstocking*, by Astrid Lindgren.

'I believe that once in a while we all need to try something that makes us a bit afraid or uncomfortable. For me, it was things like giving a speech in front of 1,000 people. Doing live TV for the first time. Or just taking on a new job or task I'd never done before.'

Today, Lisa lives in an old rectory in the countryside near Falkenberg with her husband, Marcus Nordgren (also a chef), their two children, two cats, lots of chickens and about 180,000 bees. Oh yes, and the award-winning restaurant, Prostens Pizza, in the garden. What happened?

Says Lisa, 'This is the interesting thing about dreaming. I'd always been a planner and I do still love lists and planning. What I now know is that it's also extremely important to make room for the unplanned, impulsive and spontaneous. Responding to the advertisement for the old rectory was when magic happened for us.'

Awards, international recognition and even a new prime-time television series are not the main thing for Lisa. She's followed her passions, reimagined her dreams as they've changed and has now dreamed up an idyllic life with her family that brings together all her passions. There are lessons there for all of us.

Let Lisa's story inspire you to discover and follow your passion. Take some time now while it's fresh in your mind to ponder on it and, in the space below, or in your Dream Life Journal, write down anything you've learnt that you could apply in your own life.

WHEN YOUR VALUES ARE

CLEAR TO YOU, MAKING

DECISIONS IS EASIER.

- ROY E. DISNEY -

CHAPTER SEVEN

BE GUIDED BY WHAT YOU TRULY VALUE

What you value is a reflection of who you are as a person. These things are unique to you so understanding them is a great place to start when planning to make your dream life a reality.

Why? Because when you are dreaming, setting goals or making big decisions, having a clear understanding and simple list of what you truly value – in writing – keeps you focused on what is truly important and simplifies your decisions. Your dream life is very likely to be one where you are guided strongly by what you truly value.

A person I have been inspired by immensely is Michelle Obama, a woman of such substance and style who has lived a life of meaning and accomplishment on the world stage after growing up in a hard-working blue collar family on the South Side of Chicago. She built a career in law before trading it for a career in public service working to empower young people, juggling the demands of motherhood and work, and eventually becoming the first African-American First Lady.

The way I see it, Michelle Obama's life is one that is very much guided by strong values that, I'll think you'll agree, seem to start at home for her and guide her actions across other parts of her life too. In her own words: 'It really comes down to the values of fairness and equality we want to pass down to our girls. These are basic values that children learn at a very young age and that we encourage them to apply in all areas of their lives. And in a country where we teach our children that everyone is equal under the law, discriminating against same-sex couples just isn't right. It's as simple as that.'[10]

My take on this quote is that the values of fairness and equality she talks about above have also been a strong driving force behind her campaign for girls across the globe to have access to education. Her aim is to empower millions, in the same way she was empowered by her own education, as you'll see in the message she delivered at the Global Citizen Festival in New York City on 23rd September 2017:

---

10 CULP-RESSLER, TARA. 'MICHELLE OBAMA SUPPORTS MARRIAGE EQUALITY SO THAT "EVERYONE IS EQUAL UNDER THE LAW".' THINK PROGRESS, JUNE 1, 2012, HTTPS://THINKPROGRESS.ORG/MICHELLE-OBAMA-SUPPORTS-MARRIAGE-EQUALITY-SO-THAT-EVERYONE-IS-EQUAL-UNDER-THE-LAW-91642F63FEBB/

'Today, 130 million girls of all ages are still not in school. This breaks my heart, both as a woman whose life was transformed by my education and as the mother of two daughters who wants them and every girl on this planet to fulfil her boundless potential and become who and what she is meant to be. So while times change and I may no longer live in the White House, I have no intention of walking away from these girls.'

She is a great example of how we can all be guided in our own ways by what we truly value as we reimagine our futures via our dreams.

Every year, I take time out to revisit my list of what I value, review how my life is going against each item, and then dream and set goals for each of them again. Over the years, I've refined my list to six things I value most. I could focus on more, but I've found that keeping my list to five or six is most helpful for me. That said, some people I know happily and productively use up to ten.

I've included my top six below in case it helps you. I've adjusted this list over the years when it's felt right to do so, reflecting the fact that what I value changes and evolves as my life does.

WHAT I VALUE MOST

- + FAMILY AND HOME
- + PERSONAL DEVELOPMENT AND ALL THINGS TO IMPROVE MY LIFE
- + HEALTH AND WELLNESS
- + TRAVEL
- + SHARING, INSPIRING AND EMPOWERING OTHERS
- + KIKKI.K

A note of explanation. There are many things I value highly that aren't on this list. Things like honesty and integrity, fairness, equality – and many more. For me those things are fundamental and inherently drive how I act in every way, so on my list I simply highlight areas I want to focus on to guide my dreaming and decision-making.

There are many books and methods out there on how to work out what you value most. I've tried quite a few and found some very complicated so I'm going to suggest a few ways that I've found to be simple, practical and useful.

For me, the most effective place to start is to look closely at where I'm spending most of my time, energy and money. Reflecting on this can give you great clues as to what you value because it shows what you prioritise naturally.

We'll explore this in an exercise at the end of this chapter, but for now, let me explain a little more. This approach is inspired by the work done by Dr John Demartini and I found his online tool[11] for Value Determination to be particularly useful. In it, he puts forward thirteen questions that will get you thinking in a whole new way about what matters to you most.

When I came across the Demartini method and spent time thinking about his questions, I initially thought that 'learning' was a core value for me because I spend so much time and money doing that. Digging deeper over time, I realised that category was too broad. I love learning, but I don't like learning about all things in life – for example, I don't like learning about maths, but I love learning about anything that has to do with living my dream life.

I realised that 'personal development' – learning about myself and how I can grow to be my best me, for myself and for others in my life – was a better way to define one of the things I value very highly. I realised that I always, always find the time, money and energy to develop myself, whether it's through books, seminars, online courses, podcasts or just asking people how they live their best life.

And this applies to all areas of my life, not just business. I devour any books that encourage me to lead my dream life. Reading about inspiring people and listening to great podcasts also helps me learn about what matters to others and how this underpins their achievements.

A note of caution: you may find this method highlights some things that you currently spend time, money or energy on that *are not in line with what really matters to you*. Not to panic – simply see this as a chance to refocus on the things that do matter.

---

11 DR JOHN DEMARTINI – PERFORMANCE AND BEHAVIOR SPECIALIST, DEMARTINI INSTITUTE, 2018. HTTPS:// DRDEMARTINI.COM/VALUE_DETERMINATION/DETERMINE_YOUR_VALUES

The second way that may help you identify what you care about is simply to go through a long checklist of values and highlight the ones that truly resonate for you. The key thing is to think about what are the top five or six values that are important in your life today or that you *want* to be important in your life in the future.

Finally, another way is to just write down a big long list of what you think your important values might be. By brainstorming – remember, no constraints – you can tap into some of the things that you hold dear, but perhaps have neglected. This list can be as long as you like; you'll trim it down later.

We're going to have a go at all three approaches next, thereby casting the net as wide as possible. Then we'll spend a little time refining, grouping and culling that list down to the five or six things that are most important to you.

UNCOVERING WHAT MATTERS MOST TO YOU IS AN EXERCISE IN PROGRESS, NOT PERFECTION.

You can refine and evolve your list over time – I certainly have – so it doesn't have to be perfect from the start. You'll know you've hit on the elements that are right for you as you work with them and they feel just right – at any given point in time – and become the foundation of your dream life.

My partner Paul started out with twelve values on his list and worked with those for a few years before whittling them down to ten (which he still feels is too many and it's a work in progress for him to reduce it further). He started out with 'Travel' as one of his values and 'Adventure' as another, and over time that became 'Travel and Adventure' (one value), as he realised that those two values went hand in hand for him. Travel was mainly about going on the adventures he loves – surfing and snowboarding.

The first time I started looking at my own values, more than a decade ago, was really good for me. In part, this was because it helped me get clarity on what to say 'no' to. My highest value at the time was my business, kikki.K – building the business was all consuming and so, so fun. Back then, I found it difficult to say no to invitations from friends to parties and events. I felt torn – wanting to chase my dream for kikki.K and also wanting to enjoy myself and to be a good friend.

In the process of thinking through what I valued, I realised that my social life was less important to me than my other values. Discovering that one fact made it easier for me to happily say no to things like social outings, dinners and events. It made it so much easier for me to make decisions.

That was years ago and now my values have evolved. Today, my highest value is 'Family and Home'. kikki.K is still in my top values, but you can see how my values have changed with my life.

One sure way of knowing whether something is right for you is the strength of the feeling you get if you neglect that part of your life. You'll feel really out of balance. As if something is missing. On the other hand, you'll know that you are focusing on the things that matter to you when they are at the heart of what you're doing when life feels fantastic.

When I discovered that one of the things I valued most was personal development, I felt great about spending time and money on books, resources, courses and seminars. Writing this down on my list of values – which I refer to regularly – inspired and motivated me to learn even more.

Now, because it's on my What I Value List, every year I plan for and focus specifically on personal development (along with my other key values). I also check in with myself regularly to see if I'm genuinely living by the important things on that list.

So, let's get stuck into the exercises on the following spread. Try to use one- or two-word answers. As with all of these exercises, be totally honest with yourself and don't write down things based on the expectations or judgements of others. There is no such thing as a wrong answer!

If you need inspiration, look back at the work you did exploring your passions in chapter 6 and see what common themes you can identify. These are likely to be related closely to the things you value most highly.

EXERCISE

01 /

REFLECT ON YOUR LAST TWELVE MONTHS. THINK ABOUT HOW YOU SPENT YOUR TIME AND ENERGY. IN PARTICULAR, THINK ABOUT HOW A NORMAL WEEK IN THAT YEAR LOOKED. NOW WRITE DOWN ANSWERS TO THE QUESTIONS BELOW – IN ONLY ONE OR TWO WORDS – AND WE'LL SORT THROUGH THE ANSWERS LATER. JUST DUMP WHATEVER COMES TO MIND. (YOU MAY ALSO WANT TO USE DR DEMARTINI'S ONLINE TOOL FOR VALUE DETERMINATION, AS MENTIONED EARLIER. IT'S REALLY USEFUL.)

+ WHAT DO YOU CURRENTLY LOVE TO SPEND YOUR TIME AND ENERGY DOING?
+ WHAT DO YOU ALWAYS MAKE TIME FOR, NO MATTER WHAT? E.G. EATING HEALTHILY
+ WHAT ARE YOU DOING WHEN YOU TOTALLY LOSE TRACK OF TIME?
+ WHAT DO YOU ACTUALLY SPEND MOST OF YOUR TIME, ENERGY AND MONEY ON? E.G. RAISING YOUR FAMILY, CREATING A BEAUTIFUL HOME, TRAVEL, ETC.
+ WHAT ARE THE THINGS YOU VALUE HIGHLY RIGHT NOW AND THE THINGS YOU PRIORITISE NATURALLY?
+ WHAT DO YOU DO THAT GIVES YOU THE MOST ENERGY AND JOY?
+ WHAT THINGS DO YOU SURROUND YOURSELF WITH, AT HOME AND AT WORK? E.G. FLOWERS, MUSIC, FRIENDS, ETC.
+ WHAT INSPIRES YOU?
+ WHAT DO YOU WISH YOU COULD SPEND MORE TIME DOING?
+ WHAT THINGS DO YOU DO NOW THAT YOU LOVE, AND WILL CONTINUE DOING IN YOUR DREAM LIFE?
+ IS THERE ANYTHING YOU'RE SPENDING SIGNIFICANT TIME, MONEY AND ENERGY ON THAT IS DESTRUCTIVE, THAT MAKES YOU FEEL UNCOMFORTABLE WHEN YOU THINK ABOUT IT, OR IS A BIG DISTRACTION AND WASTE OF TIME?
+ IF THOSE THINGS ABOVE ARE THINGS YOU'D REALLY LIKE TO CHANGE, WHAT ARE THE VALUES THAT ARE DRIVING YOUR DESIRE FOR CHANGE?

WHEN YOU CAN'T THINK OF ANY MORE, REVIEW YOUR LIST AND TRY TO GROUP THEM INTO NO MORE THAN FIVE OR SIX THEMES. THESE WILL PROBABLY APPEAR QUITE NATURALLY – FOR EXAMPLE, YOUR RELATIONSHIPS WITH YOUR PARTNER AND CHILDREN, PARENTS AND FRIENDS COULD BE GROUPED SIMPLY UNDER 'FAMILY AND FRIENDS'.

---

02 /

GO THROUGH THE LIST ON THE OPPOSITE PAGE AND HIGHLIGHT FIVE OR SIX WORDS – NO MORE THAN TEN – THAT TRULY RESONATE FOR YOU AS THINGS THAT ARE ALREADY IMPORTANT IN YOUR LIFE OR THAT YOU WANT TO BE VERY IMPORTANT IN YOUR LIFE.

EXERCISE

ACHIEVEMENT / ADVENTURE / ART / AUTHENTICITY / BALANCE /

BEAUTY / BOLDNESS / BUSINESS / CAREER / CHALLENGE / CHANGE /

CITIZENSHIP / COMFORT / COMMUNICATION / COMMUNITY /

COMPASSION / CONTRIBUTION / CREATIVITY / CULTURE / CURIOSITY /

DESIGN / DETERMINATION / EMPATHY / ENERGY / ENVIRONMENT /

EQUALITY / FAIRNESS / FAITH / FAME / FAMILY / FINANCIAL

FREEDOM / FREEDOM / FRIENDSHIPS / FUN / GROWTH / HAPPINESS /

HEALTH / HOBBIES / HONESTY / HUMOUR / INFLUENCE /

INNER HARMONY / INSPIRATION / INTEGRITY / INTIMACY /

INVESTING / JUSTICE / KINDNESS / KNOWLEDGE / LEADERSHIP /

LEARNING / LEGACY / LEISURE / LOVE / LOYALTY / MEANINGFUL

WORK / MUSIC / NATURE / OPENNESS / OPTIMISM / PARENTING /

PARTNERING / PEACE / PLEASURE / RECOGNITION / RECREATION /

RELATIONSHIPS / REPUTATION / RESPECT / RESPONSIBILITY / SECURITY /

SELF-RESPECT / SERVICE / SPIRITUALITY / STABILITY / STATUS /

SUCCESS / SUSTAINABILITY / TRAVEL / TRUST / UNIQUE EXPERIENCES /

EXERCISE

03 /

BRAINSTORM AND WRITE DOWN ANYTHING THAT YOU FEEL IS MISSING FROM THE VALUES THAT YOU'VE WRITTEN OR HIGHLIGHTED IN THE PREVIOUS STEPS – VALUES THAT YOU FEEL STRONGLY ABOUT. IF POSSIBLE, USE ONLY ONE- OR TWO-WORD DESCRIPTIONS.

---

04 /

NOW LOOK OVER ALL OF THE VALUES YOU'VE WRITTEN OR HIGHLIGHTED IN THE PREVIOUS THREE STEPS.

+ SORT AND EDIT THEM DOWN TO FIVE OR SIX KEY VALUES AND WRITE THOSE IN THE TABLE ON THE OPPOSITE PAGE OR IN YOUR DREAM LIFE JOURNAL. USE SIMPLE WORDS – OR IF IT'S MORE MEANINGFUL TO YOU, USE SIMPLE STATEMENTS LIKE 'A SENSE OF ADVENTURE' RATHER THAN JUST USING THE WORD 'ADVENTURE'. IF SOME THEMES OR TOPICS GO HAND IN HAND FOR YOU, YOU CAN ALSO JOIN THESE TOGETHER TO SIMPLIFY YOUR LIST. FOR EXAMPLE, I JOINED 'FAMILY AND HOME' INTO ONE VALUE BECAUSE, FOR ME, THEY BELONG TOGETHER. THERE'S NO RIGHT OR WRONG HERE.
+ IN THE COLUMN NEXT TO EACH, WRITE DOWN YOUR 'WHY?' FOR EACH. WHY IS EACH OF THESE IMPORTANT ENOUGH TO BE ON YOUR LIST? REMEMBER, THEY NEED TO BE AUTHENTIC AND RIGHT FOR YOU.
+ WE'LL REFER BACK TO YOUR FINAL LIST OF VALUES AHEAD IN CHAPTER 12 WHEN YOU START DREAMING BY LIFE AREA AND BY YOUR KEY VALUES.

TAKE YOUR TIME WITH THIS. YOU MIGHT WANT TO WRITE YOUR LIST OF VALUES OVER SEVERAL DAYS – WITH THINKING TIME IN BETWEEN – AND BE FLEXIBLE ENOUGH TO ADJUST IT OVER TIME UNTIL THE LIST FEELS JUST RIGHT FOR YOU. KEEP THE LIST CLOSE AND LOOK AT IT OFTEN, PARTICULARLY WHEN MAKING BIG DECISIONS, TO KEEP YOUR FOCUS ON WHAT IS TRULY IMPORTANT TO YOU.

ONCE YOU'VE IDENTIFIED WHAT YOU VALUE MOST, DON'T THROW AWAY YOUR ORIGINAL LONG LISTS AND THE OTHER WORK YOU'VE DONE HERE. IT'LL BE GREAT TO REFER BACK TO THESE OVER TIME AS YOU REFLECT ON THE DREAM LIFE YOU'RE CREATING. AS I SAID EARLIER, I FIND IT REALLY WORTHWHILE TO DO THIS EXERCISE ANNUALLY.

EXERCISE

MY VALUES	WHY?

BE GUIDED BY WHAT YOU TRULY VALUE

1 WHAT MATTERS MOST TO YOU –
WHAT YOU TRULY VALUE –
IS A REFLECTION OF
WHO YOU ARE

2 WHEN YOU KNOW WHAT YOU
VALUE MOST HIGHLY, YOU CAN
CHOOSE TO SAY YES TO THE
RIGHT THINGS AND NO TO THINGS
THAT ARE LESS IMPORTANT

3 MAKE TIME TO EXPLORE WHAT
MATTERS TO YOU AND THEN
PRIORITISE THESE PARTS OF
YOUR LIFE SO YOU CAN LIVE
WITH GREATER BALANCE,
JOY AND PURPOSE

4 LET WHAT YOU
TRULY VALUE GUIDE
YOUR DREAMING

LET WHAT YOU TRULY VALUE

GUIDE YOU – OR BE DRIVEN BY THE

HUSTLE AND BUSTLE OF LIFE,

THE DEMANDS OF OTHERS AND

THE VAGARIES OF CIRCUMSTANCE.

THE CHOICE IS YOURS.

– ANON. –

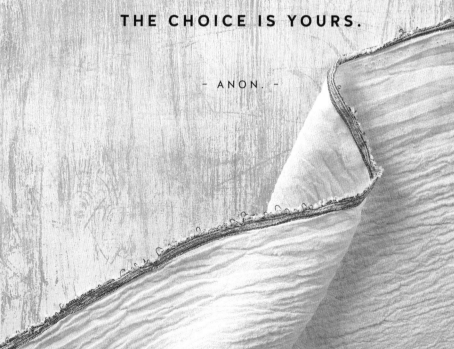

A LIFE OF DREAMS DRIVEN BY VALUES

STELLA MCCARTNEY, OBE

When I started thinking about someone whose values underpin her dreams, Stella McCartney was the first name that came to my mind and I'm so grateful she agreed I could share insights on that with you here.

Famous since birth, due to her parents – ex-Beatle Paul McCartney and his late wife, Linda – Stella spent much of her early life travelling the world with her parents' new band, Wings. When that finished, the family returned to England to rural Sussex, where she led a remarkably down-to-earth childhood, attending the local state school and helping out around the family's organic farm.

Now one of the most famous fashion designers in the world, Stella's career was launched in glittering style in 1995 when her friends Kate Moss and Naomi Campbell strode the runway in her clothes for her graduation ceremony at Central Saint Martins' College of Art and Design in London. Just two years later, she was hired in the dream role of Head Designer at the fashion house, Chloé.

Critics were quick to claim her meteoric rise was down to her family name. When it was announced in 1997 that Stella would be taking the role at Chloé, Chanel's Karl Lagerfeld took a swipe at her. 'Chloé should have taken a big name,' he said. 'They did, but in music, not fashion. Let's hope she's as gifted as her father.'

But Karl and other critics were silenced when customers and the industry clearly disagreed. She received the VH1/Vogue Designer of the Year Award in 2000 just five years after graduating and, since then, Karl has reputedly sent many letters to Stella, begging her to come to tea.

But as fabulous as Stella's creations are – and I absolutely love my Stella bag – it's the way she is so genuinely driven by her values and how they guide the way she shapes her future that I find so, so inspiring.

'The beliefs I was raised with – to respect animals and to be aware of nature, to understand that we share this planet with other creatures – have had a huge impact on me,' she told *The Guardian* in 2009.[12]

EVERYONE CAN DO SIMPLE THINGS TO MAKE A DIFFERENCE AND EVERY LITTLE BIT REALLY DOES COUNT.

Stella is a lifelong vegetarian – like her mother, Linda – and alongside her father, Paul, and her sister, Mary McCartney, started Meat Free Monday, a not-for-profit campaign that aims to raise awareness of the environmental impact of eating meat and encourage people to slow climate change, preserve natural resources and improve their health by having at least one meat-free day each week.

She uses every opportunity to speak out against animal cruelty and for the environment, both issues close to my heart too.

None of her collections ever use leather or fur. Her skincare and perfume ranges are organic. Even packaging for her new range of socks uses 100 per cent biodegradable plastic – her contribution towards tackling the massive problem of plastic waste.

And that's just the start. The campaigning eco-crusader only uses viscose sourced from sustainable forests, cashmere from leftover fibres and recycled nylon fabric in her sensational Falabella bags.

'We believe no materials should be wasted, instead being turned back into raw material, greatly reducing the need for virgin fibres that use up our planet's resources' is the company's credo.

---

12 JESS CARTNER-MORLEY, 'STELLA MCCARTNEY: "FASHION PEOPLE ARE PRETTY HEARTLESS", GUARDIAN (LONDON, UK), OCTOBER 4, 2009, HTTPS://WWW.THEGUARDIAN.COM/LIFEANDSTYLE/2009/OCT/05/STELLA-MCCARTNEY-FASHION-HEARTLESS

Her new passion is for what she calls 'circularity' and I encourage you to look at her website[13] to find out more about it. Essentially, it's a wake-up call for the fashion industry – and us as consumers – to change our wasteful ways.

Some of the facts at her fingertips are horrifying. One truckload of textiles goes into landfill every second. In the last fifteen years, we've doubled the amount of clothes we produce and now they're only worn an average of three times before they're thrown away.

At a sold-out event at the Victoria and Albert Museum in November 2017 for the Ellen MacArthur Foundation,[14] she gave an impassioned speech to outline a plan for a waste-free, circular textiles economy. 'We call on the entire industry, brands and customers to come together and fundamentally change the system.'

And that is one of the things I love about Stella. She's not only brilliant at what she does professionally, but she also uses her values as the guiding force behind everything she does and to inform the future she wants to create for herself, her children and the world.

Her dream for our world is a big one and her story provides great inspiration for how we can all use our own unique values to shape our own dreams.

Let Stella's story inspire you to be guided by what you truly value. Take some time now while it's fresh in your mind to ponder on it and, in the space provided, or in your Dream Life Journal, write down anything you've learnt that you could apply in your own life.

13 STELLA MCCARTNEY, 2018. HTTPS://WWW.STELLAMCCARTNEY.COM/EXPERIENCE/US/SUSTAINABILITY/CIRCULARITY-2/
14 ELLEN MACARTHUR FOUNDATION, 2018. HTTPS://WWW.ELLENMACARTHURFOUNDATION.ORG/

CHOOSE A JOB YOU LOVE AND

YOU'LL NEVER HAVE TO WORK

A DAY IN YOUR LIFE.

- ANON. -

CHAPTER EIGHT

LIFE IS SHORT – LIVE WITHOUT REGRET

YOUR DREAM LIFE STARTS HERE

As long as I can remember, I've always felt that life is short. The days fly by and every year seems to move faster. Do you feel that sometimes too? It's one of the reasons why I believe it's so important for us all to really take the time to think intentionally about what we want our dream life to be so that we can create a clear path to follow.

The Top Five Regrets of the Dying: A Life Transformed by the Dearly Departing is a truly moving and inspiring book by Bronnie Ware[15] and well worth reading. Bronnie worked in palliative care for many years and she captured what she learnt and her experiences with her patients in the book. Among them, she noted that the top five regrets of her dying patients were:

1. I wish I'd had the courage to live a life true to myself, not the life others expected of me.

2. I wish I didn't work so hard, and so much.

3. I wish I'd had the courage to express my feelings more.

4. I wish I'd been better at staying in touch with my friends.

5. I wish that I had let myself be happier.

The one statement from the list above that clearly resonates with me is about working so hard. It's something I am always very conscious of as I do think about work a lot. Right now, one of the things I'm working on is to be better at switching off from work when I'm at home. This means not checking emails and being more present with my family. I can't give myself a tick as being perfect yet, but the right habit is forming as I'm moving towards living the way I want to live. It's all about progress and not perfection, after all.

---

15 BRONNIE WARE, *THE TOP FIVE REGRETS OF THE DYING: A LIFE TRANSFORMED BY THE DEARLY DEPARTING* (CARLSBAD, CA: HAY HOUSE, 2012)

So, which statements from the list above resonate with you? There is so much to learn from people who are approaching the end of their lives, and these statements are a great reminder of the importance of living your own authentic life. A life you can look back on and be proud of, where you can say that you were true to your values, passions and dreams.

LIVE A LIFE WITH NO REGRETS.

Often it's in moments when we're exposed to death, tragedy or tough circumstances that we humans feel our mortality and finally understand what is truly important to us. This is the silver lining around the cloud of unfortunate circumstances and the exercises in this chapter are about how you can tap into the concept of regret to gain a unique perspective into your dreams so you can intentionally shape your future.

It's so easy to get caught up spending time and energy on things that, when you stop and think about it, aren't really that important to you or aren't truly in line with your values. I often hear people talk about being in jobs they don't enjoy or in relationships that are toxic.

IF SOMEONE TOLD YOU HOW MANY HOURS, DAYS, WEEKS AND YEARS YOU HAD LEFT TO LIVE, WOULD THAT CHANGE THE WAY YOU LIVE?

How would you feel if you knew you had only three years left? What if it was only one year? What would you make more time for? What would you do with your life?

I find thinking about the time I have left and how I want to use it really focuses my mind. I don't want to waste my time. I don't want to spend it doing things that I don't believe in.

I don't want to compromise on my values. I want to be the best person I can be, living a life I love and making a contribution to the lives of others.

If you live to be 100 years old, you will have 1,200 months to live in total.

A great thing to do now is to work out how many months you might have left to do everything you want to do in your life. Simply subtract your age from 100, then multiply that number by twelve to give you a rough idea.

For example, that means someone who is thirty years old now has 840 months to go. It doesn't seem like much, but I find it so inspiring to think about what I want to do with those years, months, weeks and days in order to make the most of my life. Take a moment to calculate that now for yourself and write the numbers below.

100 years old minus my age today of _____ = _____ x 12 = _____ months ahead for me!

How does this make you feel? Some people tell me they find this a little morbid, but I find it to be the exact opposite. It's so powerful, so inspiring and so worth doing.

I recently shared the concept with a twenty-two-year-old friend of mine, who is currently at university and not exactly sure what to do with her life. Her response was passionate and excited. 'I've never stopped before to think about the fact that my time is limited. I love understanding that,' she said. 'I've been thinking about living overseas and it prompted me to discuss the idea with my mother. She told me I had to follow my heart.'

The undeniable fact is we will all die at some point, so my recommendation is to accept the truth and let it inspire us to make the most of this one precious life we all have.

A few months ago, I led dinner guests through the 101 Dreams exercise during an evening I hosted. I love the example of one friend who had founded and grown a wonderful business and had been busy for years making that dream happen, before selling it to embrace other things in life. I just loved one of the dreams she shared for this new stage of her life, which was to buy a sewing machine to rediscover the simple joy of creating with her own hands.

Tap into your heart, think about what it is that you do not want to regret. Think about what's truly important to you *and* what's not important at this stage of your life. Take those learnings on board as you imagine how your dream life looks. A full and happy life – one without regrets.

EXERCISE

IN YOUR DREAM LIFE JOURNAL:

01 /

THINK ABOUT THE FIVE COMMON REGRETS OF THE DYING YOU READ EARLIER IN THIS CHAPTER.
RE-READ THEM.

+ DO ANY OF THEM RESONATE WITH YOU RIGHT NOW? WHICH ONES? WHY?
+ WHAT SIMPLE ACTIONS COULD YOU TAKE RIGHT NOW TO AVOID REGRETS AND MOVE YOU CLOSER
  TOWARDS YOUR DREAM LIFE?

02 /

IF YOU KNEW YOU WERE GOING TO DIE IN THREE YEARS FROM NOW – AND THAT YOU WOULD LIVE
WITH PERFECT HEALTH UNTIL THEN...

QUESTION	ANSWER
WHAT WOULD YOU DO WITH YOUR REMAINING YEARS?	
WHAT WOULD YOU START DOING?	
WHAT WOULD YOU STOP DOING?	
WHAT WOULD BE THE THEME OF THOSE THREE YEARS?	

EXERCISE

NOW TAKE A COLOURED PEN AND CIRCLE YOUR ANSWERS THAT WOULD APPLY IF THOSE THREE YEARS WERE REDUCED TO JUST TWELVE MONTHS. THIS SHOULD GIVE YOU REAL CLARITY ON THE MOST IMPORTANT THINGS TO YOU...

QUESTION	ANSWER
WHAT WOULD BE THE THEME OF THOSE TWELVE MONTHS?	

03 /

FOR THIS LAST EXERCISE IN THIS CHAPTER, YOU'LL NEED TO STOP AND TAKE A DEEP BREATH. CLEAR YOUR MIND AND TAP INTO YOUR IMAGINATION AND YOUR HEART. OUR REASON FOR DOING THIS EXERCISE IS TO GIVE YOU A SLIGHTLY DIFFERENT PERSPECTIVE ON REGRET - IN FACT, I WANT YOU TO MOVE PAST REGRET AND IMAGINE THAT YOU'RE LIVING A LIFE WITHOUT REGRET.

NOW, IN YOUR MIND, LEAN INTO THE FUTURE AND IMAGINE YOURSELF AT NINETY YEARS OF AGE. YOU LOOK WELL, HEALTHY, HAPPY, CALM AND WISE. IMAGINE YOUR WRINKLES. YOUR DISTINGUISHED GREY HAIR. LOOK AT THE TWINKLE IN YOUR NINETY-YEAR-OLD EYES. REALLY FEEL WHAT IT'S LIKE TO BE YOU AT NINETY.

NOW THAT YOU ARE YOUR NINETY-YEAR-OLD SELF, THINK ABOUT AND WRITE YOUR ANSWER TO THE FOLLOWING QUESTION:

AGAINST THE VALUES YOU IDENTIFIED IN CHAPTER 7, WHAT ACHIEVEMENTS ARE YOU MOST PROUD OF AS YOU LOOK BACK OVER YOUR WONDERFUL LIFE?

OVER THE NEXT FEW DAYS, PONDER ON YOUR ANSWERS TO THE ABOVE QUESTIONS. ADD ANYTHING ELSE THAT COMES TO MIND. COLLECTIVELY, THE ANSWERS AND THOUGHTS YOU'VE WRITTEN IN THIS CHAPTER'S EXERCISES WILL GIVE YOU SOME GREAT CLUES AS TO WHAT IS MOST IMPORTANT TO YOU WHEN THE HUSTLE AND BUSTLE OF DAY-TO-DAY LIFE IS STRIPPED AWAY.

WHAT YOU HAVE IN FRONT OF YOU NOW IS A GREAT PLACE FOR YOU TO FOCUS AND IT'LL GIVE YOU WONDERFUL INPUT TO LOOK BACK ON LATER IN YOUR JOURNEY TOWARDS CREATING YOUR DREAM LIFE.

BEFORE MOVING ON TO THE NEXT CHAPTER, TAKE TIME TO THINK THROUGH ANYTHING THAT'S COME UP HERE FOR YOU THAT YOU WANT TO ADD TO YOUR 101 DREAMS LIST - AND GO ADD IT.

LIFE IS SHORT - LIVE WITHOUT REGRET

1 DON'T WASTE YOUR TIME LIVING A LIFE LIMITED BY SOMEONE ELSE'S EXPECTATIONS OR THOSE OF SOCIETY

2 LIVE A LIFE THAT IS AUTHENTIC TO YOU - GUIDED BY YOUR OWN VALUES, PASSIONS AND SENSE OF PURPOSE

3 NONE OF US KNOW HOW LONG WE HAVE TO LIVE SO TAKE ACTION TODAY TO MAKE EVERY DAY COUNT

THE TIME WILL PASS ANYWAY. YOU

CAN EITHER SPEND IT CREATING

THE LIFE YOU WANT, OR SPEND IT

LIVING THE LIFE YOU DON'T WANT.

THE CHOICE IS YOURS.

- ANON. -

BRINGING DREAMS TO LIFE

YVONNE HALLGREN

O f all the amazing dreams I've heard over the years, it was hearing the story of my dear friend, Yvonne, that made me realise how powerfully dreams can inspire people to courageously and fiercely pursue what they value.

On the surface, Yvonne's dream was simple – the kind of thing many of us never think twice about. She wanted to have a child with Kim, the man she loved. Unlike most people, though, Yvonne faced some significant barriers to make her dream come true. Even writing this makes me cry...

Yvonne was just twenty-six when she discovered that she had a very rare disease, primary pulmonary hypertension. There's no cure and pregnancy can raise the blood pressure to a point that is fatal to either the mother or baby. Very few people with the disease have ever given birth.

Right from the start of their relationship, Yvonne had warned Kim about her health issues. 'I told him that I wasn't able to have children, and he deserved that opportunity as I knew he'd be a fantastic father.'

However, their relationship grew stronger and stronger, and Yvonne began to dream of a child. 'I really wanted a child with Kim. It wasn't just a child that was important to me; my entire soul and body told me that I needed to experience parenthood together with Kim,' she said.

But the decision to conceive was not made lightly. 'The dream of being parents together was so strong, I felt invincible,' said Yvonne. 'I never felt any doubt – I just had to convince the doctors to help me. I knew I'd need all their expertise and support.' The head doctor, after deep investigation of all the facts, agreed to support her dream. 'It was a relief. I had to agree to leave every decision to her and my other doctors. If they wanted to cancel the pregnancy, I had to agree. There couldn't be any doubt about that. So we were allowed to try to get pregnant.'

Family and friends also provided crucial support, although many were worried. 'They knew what I would be risking if I got pregnant.'

When Yvonne did fall pregnant, it was like a dream come true. 'I had to visit the doctor every other week, but I felt perfect. I think I had morning sickness for about ten minutes!' said Yvonne.

Then in week 25, the baby stopped moving. 'I knew right away that the baby was dead. Friends tried to reassure me, but I just knew,' she said. Yvonne's instincts had been right and two days later she gave birth to her daughter. 'I held her body in my arms and Kim and I mourned together. My heart broke. I thought I would never be happy again.'

Their family and friends were there for them in their grief. Yvonne wrote a lot in her journal. She and Kim spent a lot of time together – they talked, walked, went for car rides and tried to overcome their paralysing sorrow. But throughout it all, Yvonne never lost sight of her dream.

Within three months, Yvonne was pregnant again, both terrified and happy at the same time. As she recollects, 'We even dreamed about names. We said "it" was a soccer player, but we didn't know if it was a girl or a boy. That was not important. The baby to be was a symbol of our love for each other and a tribute to life itself.'

At week 34, it was time for Yvonne to give birth – all under the care of the thoracic medical team. There were a LOT of doctors and nurses in the room. Given that not many mothers and babies had ever survived under similar circumstances, it was a huge event for the hospital – not to mention for Yvonne and Kim.

Yvonne's first sight of her beautiful baby boy was from photos that Kim had taken before the new bub had been whisked off to a specialist children's hospital.

Twenty-one years later, Malte is now a beautiful, loving and caring young man, and Yvonne and Kim are so proud of him. 'My dream now is for Malte to be happy and to have a life partner and family of his own. Most of all, I want him to believe in himself and dare to dream.'

For herself, having just come through a *second* lung transplant – a painful and difficult ordeal that was barely describable and which she only just managed to pull through – Yvonne dreams of simply living a long and mindful life, full of joy, courage and love.

'To continue to dream ... it's as simple as that,' she says.

Let Yvonne's story inspire you to bring your dreams to life. Take some time now while it's fresh in your mind to ponder on it and, in the space below, or in your Dream Life Journal, write down anything you've learnt that you could apply in your own life.

DON'T LIVE THE SAME YEAR 75 TIMES

AND CALL IT A LIFE.

- ROBIN SHARMA -

CHAPTER NINE

THE POWER OF PURPOSE

YOUR DREAM LIFE STARTS HERE

I like to think of purpose as the motivating force that gets you out of bed in the morning ... the unique difference you have to offer the world.

Having a clear sense of your own purpose in life is exhilarating and valuable for so many reasons – particularly in informing and guiding your dreaming. For some people, it can be a long process of discovery. It can take time to refine your purpose to a point where it is really clear for you, but once you have, it'll be so helpful when crafting what your dream life might look like. Working through this chapter will give you a good start.

Other benefits of having a sense of your purpose in life include helping you deal with the many challenges and decisions that life throws your way. It gives you a sense of being part of something much bigger than yourself. You'll feel connected to something meaningful and worthwhile that gives you a strong sense that your life matters.

You'll know you are close when you find what gives you the most energy and joy. Your sense of purpose will be inspiring for people around you.

And wouldn't it be amazing if you could make a living or spend a large part of your life following your purpose and doing what you love?

A great friend of mine, Dr Libby Weaver, is a super example of this. Apart from being one of the loveliest people I know, Lib is one of the world's leading nutritional biochemists, an eleven-time bestselling author and an international speaker.

Her mission is to 'educate and inspire, enhancing people's health and happiness, and igniting a ripple effect that transforms the world'. She has pursued a career that follows her purpose, and her energy and joy as she does so is infectious for those around her.

Sharing what you care about with the world lights up both the giver and the receiver. Lib has shared with me many times that she just loves 'seeing the light return to people's eyes as they reconnect to their passions, purpose and ability to take even better care of themselves'. When you live your purpose each day, your vocation becomes more like a vacation in the daily energy it offers you and the lives you touch.

In chapter 7, we did some important work on identifying your values – the things that matter most to you. Now, we'll be exploring how these relate to your purpose.

Knowing your values helps you find your purpose. I've heard people refer to values as being like the banks of a great river – they guide the river and support its flow. The banks create a clear path for the river and, without them, the river would spread out and dissipate over the land. The river is your purpose ... the powerful force that is shaped and guided by your values.

Few people would show a strong sense of purpose more clearly than world renowned anthropologist, Dame Jane Goodall, DBE, who has made the study of chimpanzees her life's purpose and work, overcoming enormous obstacles to raise awareness of the species and save them from threat.

Think of other people you admire too, in any field of endeavour. People who've achieved amazing things in their life generally show a very strong sense of purpose, and that's what we hope to bring to light for you here.

Don't worry if you don't yet have a strong sense of what your purpose in life is. Again, this is a process and it takes time. There's no hurry. You're doing the work that will help you identify it, then you can use it to inform your dreaming.

Here's a thought for you: being frustrated by a lack of purpose can actually be a really good thing. From my personal experience – when I was lacking direction before creating my 3am List – my deep frustration became a strong catalyst for change, driving me forward to search for what my purpose in life really was.

From the stories so many people share with me, it strikes me that rather than following their own sense of purpose, many people either follow what they feel others expect, or spend much of their time reacting to circumstances or following what other people do.

Psychologists explain that this leads to feelings of emptiness. This isn't so surprising. Without having a strong reason to get out of bed in the morning, life can seem meaningless.

The Japanese have a concept relating to this – they call it '*ikigai*' – which doesn't have a direct translation into English but embodies the idea of 'having purpose for living'. The word itself is made up of the Japanese characters that mean 'life' and 'to be worthwhile'. Knowing your own purpose certainly makes life feel worthwhile.

Ikigai has come under the spotlight in recent years, as scientists have studied the amazing longevity of people living on the Japanese island of Okinawa. This island has the highest ratio of centenarians anywhere in the world, with more than 520 per every million people as of September 2016.[16]

The sense of *ikigai* that shapes their life and brings what researchers have described as 'an uncommon joy' has emerged as an explanatory factor for their longevity (along with a healthy diet, pots of green tea, a simple life in the outdoors, good friendships, a strong sense of community, and enough rest and exercise).

There are important lessons we can all learn from their example.

Of course, 'what a worthwhile life' looks like is different for each of us. We're all unique. Living with a clear sense of purpose certainly helps me to feel connected, worthwhile and fulfilled.

One of my all-time favourite quotes – I love it – is often attributed to Mark Twain, but its exact origins are unknown. No matter, it's a wonderful quote and so very true.

---

16 HECTOR GARCIA AND FRANCESC MIRALLES, *IKIGAI: THE JAPANESE SECRET TO A LONG AND HAPPY LIFE* (NEW YORK: PENGUIN BOOKS, 2017)

THE TWO MOST IMPORTANT DAYS IN YOUR LIFE ARE THE DAY YOU WERE BORN AND THE DAY YOU FIND OUT WHY.

We are going to start here by simply contemplating this: it's progress, not perfection that matters. Even if you only just start to get a feeling for what your purpose is, my experience is that any progress is really helpful.

I spent quite a bit of time exploring my own purpose a few years back. I wanted to know what I might have been put on earth to do. I knew I wanted to provide for my family, to express my creativity and do something I love. Then I explored the exercises you'll find at the end of this chapter and I discovered so much more. All of this has since been a great help to me as I've reimagined how I wanted my life to be.

I discovered that I want to inspire the world to dream – to help people be their very best, to inspire them to inspire others, and make the world a better place in the process. I also discovered that part of what gets me out of bed every day is to create and share beautiful and meaningful things with the world – things that add sparks of joy to everyday life and inspire and empower people to live their dream life, whatever that means for them.

MY PURPOSE LIST

+ PROVIDING A WONDERFUL LIFE FOR MY FAMILY
+ BEING THE BEST PARENT I CAN BE
+ CREATING AND SHARING BEAUTIFUL AND MEANINGFUL THINGS
+ HELPING THE WORLD TO DREAM

You'll notice that I've used verbs or 'doing words' to describe my purpose. There is a very good reason for this, and it all comes back to the differences between values and purpose.

One of my top values is 'Family' (and home), and my purpose in life is to *provide a wonderful life for them* (i.e. this is what I do.) This helps me so much in how I approach every day, and also when I'm dreaming for the year ahead. It helps me focus on what I need to do. If something is distracting me from that purpose, then it's a good indication that it is something I need to say no to.

A lot has been written about finding your purpose, but much of this is made very complex. My experience is to keep it really simple and the best two ways I've found are shared here for you to try for yourself. You may find it a little confronting or challenging, but I've found going through this process really helps me get clarity. I believe you'll find that too.

'IT IS GOOD TO HAVE AN END TO JOURNEY
TOWARD; BUT IT IS THE JOURNEY
THAT MATTERS, IN THE END.'

- URSULA K. LE GUIN -

EXERCISE

IN YOUR DREAM LIFE JOURNAL:

01 /

SPEND TIME REFLECTING ON WHAT IT IS THAT GETS YOU OUT OF BED EVERY DAY. IT COULD BE SEVERAL KEY THINGS. DESCRIBE EACH IN AS FEW WORDS AS POSSIBLE TO KEEP IT SIMPLE. FORCE YOURSELF TO LIMIT EACH TO FIVE OR SIX WORDS. WRITE AS MANY AS YOU CAN POSSIBLY THINK OF, THEN RANK THEM IN THE ORDER THAT MAKES THE MOST SENSE TO YOU.

IT CAN HELP TO ASK YOURSELF THE QUESTION: 'WHY WAS I PUT ON THIS EARTH?' DON'T WORRY IF NOTHING SPRINGS OUT IMMEDIATELY. KEEP AT IT OVER TIME AND TRY TO WHITTLE YOUR LIST BACK TO THREE OR FOUR POINTS THAT MAKE THE MOST SENSE TO YOU.

02 /

ANOTHER REALLY USEFUL WAY TO HELP YOU EXPLORE YOUR PURPOSE IS TO THINK OF WHAT REALLY FRUSTRATES YOU OR WHAT YOU DEFINITELY DON'T WANT TO DO. FOR EXAMPLE, IF YOU ARE DEEPLY FRUSTRATED IN YOUR CAREER - AS I WAS - THEN IT'S A GREAT INDICATION YOU'RE LIKELY NOT LIVING YOUR PURPOSE BY DOING WHAT YOU'RE DOING.

READ OPRAH'S AMAZING STORY IN THE COMING PAGES AND REFLECT ON HER SELF-KNOWLEDGE THAT SHE DIDN'T WANT HER GRANDMOTHER'S LIFE.

THINK OF WHAT DEEPLY FRUSTRATES YOU AND WHAT YOU DON'T WANT. LIST EVERYTHING, NO MATTER HOW TRIVIAL IT SEEMS, AND USE THIS LIST AS INSPIRATION TO WRITE DOWN WHAT YOUR TRUE PURPOSE MAY BE.

03 /

NOW THAT YOU'VE DONE THE TWO EXERCISES - AND YOU HAVE MORE CLARITY ON THE REASON YOU EXIST IN THIS WORLD - WRITE DOWN ANYTHING ELSE YOU WANT TO ADD TO YOUR 101 DREAMS LIST. COME BACK AND THINK OVER YOUR PURPOSE AT LEAST ONCE A YEAR (PUT A REMINDER IN YOUR DIARY NOW). REVIEW AND REFINE IT - IN WRITING OF COURSE!

THERE IS NO GREATER GIFT

YOU CAN GIVE OR RECEIVE

THAN TO HONOUR YOUR CALLING.

IT'S WHY YOU WERE BORN.

AND HOW YOU BECOME

MOST TRULY ALIVE.

- OPRAH WINFREY -

DREAM. DO. ENJOY. SHARE.

'HAPPINESS IS WHEN WHAT YOU THINK, WHAT YOU
SAY, AND WHAT YOU DO ARE IN HARMONY.'
- MAHATMA GANDHI

Some years ago, I spent a long time thinking about what my purpose was in life – why I exist, what gets me out of bed every day. It was the same process we went through together in the previous chapter. And four simple words kept coming up for me. Dream. Do. Enjoy. Share.

I realised that these four key elements help me make sense of everything I've ever done and that when they are in balance, I feel amazing and I know I'm living my dream life.

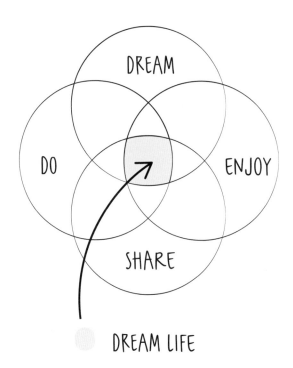

They've since become a key philosophy for me, both personally and in my business.

For me, **Dream**ing is all about taking regular time to reach into my heart to create a vivid picture of things I deeply want to make happen in the future. It's the practice we're working through together in this book.

Doing is about getting the right things done effectively. I realised early in life that dreaming without doing is just wishful thinking – and also that doing without dreaming is so limiting. Without a strong idea of your destination – a dream – you're like a ship being blown around on the ocean, driven by elements outside your control and without a compass to guide you towards where you want to go.

Dreaming and doing are great, but life needs to be enjoyed. So many times I've been asked how I've managed to not burn out as I've worked hard to chase my dreams. The answer is simple. I do lots along the way to **Enjoy** the journey every day. To refresh and re-energise. To have fun, do what I love, look after my health, and take time to laugh and enjoy life.

And I've always had a strong inclination to **Share**. More and more as I grow, I realise that being able to connect with, work with and help others is what brings true meaning and satisfaction to life. As Dr Tererai Trent's mother told her, 'Your dreams will have more meaning when they are tied to the betterment of your community.'

Uncovering these simple truths about my purpose has transformed my life, and I wish the same for you.

THE POWER OF PURPOSE

1
YOUR PURPOSE IS YOUR MISSION
IN LIFE, YOUR CALLING, THE
REASON YOU GET OUT OF BED
IN THE MORNING

2
A SENSE OF PURPOSE GIVES
YOUR LIFE MEANING AND HELPS
YOU LIVE WITH INTENTION

3
YOU HAVE THE POWER TO MAKE
A DIFFERENCE, EVEN IN THE
SMALLEST OF WAYS

10

MORE INSPIRATION –
MY FAVOURITE DREAM QUOTES

YOUR DREAM LIFE STARTS HERE

I get so much inspiration from quotes and I've collected some of my favourites about dreaming to share with you. Which ones resonate with *you*? You can add your own favourite quotes about dreaming too.

I look at my collection of quotes every morning to keep me focused on my dreams, and if you make this part of your routine too, you'll keep them as inspiration at the forefront of your mind.

+ *'Your dreams will become clear only when you can look into your own heart. Who looks outside, dreams; who looks inside, awakes.'* – C.G. Jung

DATE AND MEANING

DATE AND MEANING

+ *'The biggest adventure you can take is to live the life of your dreams.'* – Oprah Winfrey

DATE AND MEANING

DATE AND MEANING

+ *'Nothing ... is going to stop you from fulfilling your dreams. And you deserve every last one of the successes I know your will have.'* – Michelle Obama

DATE AND MEANING

DATE AND MEANING

+ *'Don't let others hijack your dreams. Be captain of your own ship and master of your own destiny.'* – Joanne Madeline Moore

DATE AND MEANING

DATE AND MEANING

+ *'It always seems impossible until it's done.'* – Nelson Mandela

DATE AND MEANING

DATE AND MEANING

+ *'Always remember, you have within you the strength, the patience, and the passion to reach for the stars to change the world.'* – Harriet Tubman

DATE AND MEANING

DATE AND MEANING

+ *'You are never too old to set another goal or to dream a new dream.'* – C.S. Lewis

DATE AND MEANING

DATE AND MEANING

INSPIRATION IS

ALL AROUND YOU.

- ANON. -

+ *'No dreamer is ever too small; no dream is ever too big.'* – Anonymous

DATE AND MEANING

DATE AND MEANING

+ *'Miracles start to happen when you give as much energy to your dreams as you do to your fears.'* – Richard Wilkins

DATE AND MEANING

DATE AND MEANING

+ *'Don't tell me the sky's the limit when there are footprints on the moon.'* – Paul Brandt

DATE AND MEANING

DATE AND MEANING

+ *'You are never given a dream without also being given the power to make it come true. You will have to work for it, however.'* – Richard Bach

DATE AND MEANING

DATE AND MEANING

+ *'Dreams are illustrations from the book your soul is writing about you.'* – Marsha Norman

DATE AND MEANING

DATE AND MEANING

+ *'Never give up on a dream just because of the time it will take to accomplish it. The time will pass anyway.'* – Earl Nightingale

DATE AND MEANING

DATE AND MEANING

+ *'Dreams come a size too big so we can grow into them.'* – Josie Bissett

DATE AND MEANING

DATE AND MEANING

+ *'Sometimes the dreams that come true are the ones you never even knew you had.'* – Alice Sebold

DATE AND MEANING

DATE AND MEANING

+ *'All our dreams can come true, if we have the courage to pursue them.'* – Walt Disney

DATE AND MEANING

DATE AND MEANING

+ *'Whatever the mind ... can conceive and believe, it can achieve.'* – Napoleon Hill

DATE AND MEANING

DATE AND MEANING

+ *'Build your own dreams, or someone else will hire you to build theirs.'* – Farrah Gray

DATE AND MEANING

DATE AND MEANING

+ *'The only limit to the height of your achievements is the reach of your dreams and your willingness to work hard for them.'* – Michelle Obama

DATE AND MEANING

DATE AND MEANING

+ *'Don't ask what the world needs. Ask what makes you come alive, and go do it. Because what the world needs is people who have come alive.'* – Howard Thurman

DATE AND MEANING

DATE AND MEANING

+ *'If you don't have a dream, how are you going to make a dream come true?'* – Oscar Hammerstein

DATE AND MEANING

DATE AND MEANING

+ *'No one has ever achieved anything from the smallest to the greatest unless the dream was dreamed first.'* – Laura Ingalls Wilder

DATE AND MEANING

DATE AND MEANING

+ *'Anything's possible if you've got enough nerve.'* – J.K. Rowling

DATE AND MEANING

DATE AND MEANING

EXERCISE

IN YOUR DREAM LIFE JOURNAL:

01 /

TAKE TIME TO READ THROUGH THE QUOTES ON THE PREVIOUS PAGES AND THEN, UNDER ANY THAT RESONATE WITH YOU, MARK THE DATE AND WHAT IT MEANS TO YOU AT THIS POINT IN TIME. DO THIS EXERCISE IN A YEAR'S TIME AND NOTE ANY CHANGES IN YOUR THINKING. MAKE A DIARY NOTE FOR YOURSELF SO YOU REMEMBER.

FOR EXAMPLE, IF YOU ARE DREAMING ABOUT TAKING CONTROL OF YOUR OWN LIFE, THEN PERHAPS THIS QUOTE WILL APPEAL TO YOU RIGHT NOW:

'Don't let others hijack your dreams.
Be captain of your own ship and master of your own destiny.'
JOANNE MADELINE MOORE

ONE YEAR DOWN THE TRACK, HAVING TAKEN MANY SMALL STEPS TOWARDS YOUR DREAMS, YOU MAY FEEL COMPLETELY DIFFERENTLY. NOTE DOWN YOUR FEELINGS ABOUT THE PROGRESS YOU'VE MADE.

HERE'S AN EXAMPLE:

'It always seems impossible until it's done.'
NELSON MANDELA

THIS QUOTE IS A REMINDER THAT TWENTY YEARS AGO I COULD NOT HAVE IMAGINED THE LIFE I HAVE NOW. THIS PROMPTS ME TO TAKE TIME TO JOURNAL AND DREAM ABOUT MY NEXT TWENTY YEARS. AND I'M GOING TO DREAM MUCH BIGGER THAN I THINK I CAN POSSIBLY ACHIEVE.

02 /

WRITE DOWN ANY OTHER QUOTES THAT ARE MEANINGFUL AND INSPIRING TO YOU ON THE OPPOSITE PAGE. YOU CAN ALSO ADD THEM TO YOUR VISION BOARD. (WE'LL BE EXPLORING THIS IN MORE DETAIL IN CHAPTER 15.)

03 /

IF ANY IDEAS COME FROM DOING THIS, ADD TO THE WORK YOU'VE DONE UP UNTIL NOW.

EXERCISE

1

BE INSPIRED BY THE WORDS
OF OTHERS

2

COLLECT QUOTES – GATHER ANY
LEARNINGS FROM THEM THAT
RESONATE WITH YOU AND APPLY
THEM TO YOUR LIFE

DREAMS GUIDED BY VALUES AND TIED TO THE BETTERMENT OF OTHERS

MICHELLE OBAMA

Michelle Obama, former First Lady of the United States, is a woman who needs little introduction. In her own right she has inspired, and continues to inspire, hundreds of millions of people around the world to be better versions of themselves and to do their bit to make the world a better place.

Earlier in the book, as you explored how to let what you value guide your dreams, I shared how I am particularly inspired by the way she so obviously lives a life guided by strong values, which start at home and guide all her actions.

Something that fascinates me in her story is the way she describes how her parents passed on to her the key values that have shaped her life, and that now guide the lives of her children and have an impact on millions through the work she does with the Obama Foundation and other initiatives she supports.

It's such a clear example of how the important people in our lives – the ones we spend much time around – influence what we value, which in turn affects how we behave and what we dream about.

As you read her story, think about who and what has shaped your values and how you are passing those values on (and to whom). Think too about how your values lead you to behave and how they are now shaping your dreams.

In her words...

'[I was] raised on the South Side of Chicago by a father who was a blue-collar city worker and a mother who stayed at home with my brother and me. My mother's love has always been a sustaining force for our family, and one of my greatest joys is seeing her integrity, her compassion and her intelligence reflected in my own daughters.

My dad was our rock. Although he was diagnosed with multiple sclerosis in his early thirties, he was our provider, our champion, our hero. As he got sicker, it got harder for him to walk, it took him longer to get dressed in the morning. But if he was in pain, he never let on. He never stopped smiling and laughing – even while struggling to button his shirt, even while using two canes to get himself across the room to give my mom a kiss. He just woke up a little earlier and worked a little harder.

He and my mom poured everything they had into me and [my brother] Craig. It was the greatest gift a child can receive: never doubting for a single minute that you're loved, and cherished, and have a place in this world. And thanks to their faith and hard work, we both were able to go on to college.

And you know, what struck me when I first met Barack was that even though he had this funny name, even though he'd grown up all the way across the continent in Hawaii, his family was so much like mine. He was raised by grandparents who were working-class folks just like my parents, and by a single mother who struggled to pay the bills just like we did. Like my family, they scrimped and saved so that he could have opportunities they never had themselves. And Barack and I were raised with so many of the same values: that you work hard for what you want in life; that your word is your bond and you do what you say you're going to do; that you treat people with dignity and respect, even if you don't know them, and even if you don't agree with them.

And Barack and I set out to build lives guided by these values and pass them on to the next generation. Because we want our children and all children ... to know that the only limit to the height of your achievements is the reach of your dreams and your willingness to work for them.'[17]

Michelle is also a shining example of someone who Dr Tererai Trent's mother would say has tied her dreams to the betterment of others – and certainly not just after she moved her family into the White House.

In 1991, she took the decision to give up her career in law – a career she had studied and worked tremendously hard for – to change direction into a career in public service and on to working to empower young people. To improve the lives of others.

---

17 MICHELLE OBAMA, 'DEMOCRATIC NATIONAL CONVENTION KEYNOTE ADDRESS' (SPEECH, INVESCO FIELD AT MILE HIGH STADIUM, DENVER, COLORADO, AUGUST 25, 2008), AMERICAN RHETORIC, HTTP://WWW.AMERICANRHETORIC. COM/SPEECHES/CONVENTION2008/MICHELLEOBAMA2008DNC.HTM

Post-life in the White House, the former First Lady has continued to tie her dreams to the betterment of others through her involvement in setting up the Obama Foundation, with a mission to inspire and empower people to change their world in what they call 'an experiment in citizenship for the 21st century'.[18] The foundation's aim is to equip civic innovators, young leaders and everyday citizens with the skills and tools they need to create change in their communities.

She also continues to throw her support behind the dream of helping 130 million girls of all ages across the world – girls currently blocked from learning – to get an education. She knows how her own life was transformed by education and, as the mother of two daughters, she wants them and every girl on this planet to fulfil their boundless potential and become who and what they are meant to be.

It's a big dream that connects her to the dreams of Dr Tererai Trent, who wants to bring education to children in Zimbabwe. In some way it's a dream that crosses over and connects with my own: to inspire 101 million people the world over to dream. No doubt there are millions who dream of an education – for themselves or for their children.

Let Michelle Obama's story of using her voice to empower others inspire you to dream, to tie your dreams in some way to the betterment of others and to find the courage to become whoever you aspire to be.

Take some time now while it's fresh in your mind to ponder on it and, in the space below, or in your Dream Life Journal, write down anything you've learnt from her story that you could apply in your own life.

18 OBAMA FOUNDATION. 'OUR MISSION', 2018. HTTPS://WWW.OBAMA.ORG/MISSION/

ALL GLORY COMES FROM

DARING TO BEGIN.

- EUGENE F. WARE -

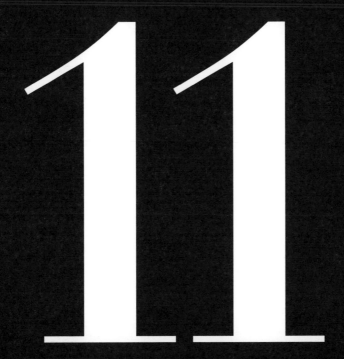

11

YOUR DREAM WEEK AND DREAM YEAR

YOUR DREAM LIFE STARTS HERE

I love thinking about what my dream week and dream year could look like. I especially love it because it gives you a different perspective on dreaming and imagining your dream life – one that can be quite practical.

Sometimes big dreams can seem unattainable, but if you stop to think about what your dream week or year looks like, it can seem so much more achievable. You start to see the small changes you could make every day, week, month and year to live your dream life.

My favourite day of the week is Sunday. On Sundays we rarely have anything booked. We keep it free to enjoy a day off, re-energise and just do whatever we feel like doing.

A dream Sunday for me starts early, around 5am, after a good night's sleep and before the rest of the family gets up. I spend the first hour writing, thinking and dreaming. I'll do some meditation and I love to go for a walk in nature too. Later in the day I'll spend hours in front of the fire, with lots of candles lit nearby, reading and drinking endless cups of tea.

I love having this time for myself – mixed with play and games with the children – while my family is around doing the things they love too. I end the day by cooking a beautiful healthy dinner and then have an early night, reading in bed. That might seem boring to some, and it certainly doesn't unfold like that every Sunday (sometimes I LOVE sleeping in), but it's my dream Sunday and when I think about how my dream life looks, Sundays look just like that.

Yours may be very different and you'll soon get the chance to let your mind wander and start imagining for yourself...

A while ago, I read *The 4-Hour Work Week* by Timothy Ferriss.[19] I knew I didn't want to work only four hours a week, but I wondered what it would look and feel like to work just a few hours a day? At the time I was working long hours and a four-hour day seemed unachievable. Today, I still don't work a four-hour day, but because I took time to contemplate the possibility of doing that, I learnt so much. As a result, I reorganised my schedule and started doing things like using time commuting to listen to podcasts or to make work phone calls. And now? I'm much closer to having my dream work week and out of the process I created more dreams for how I want to spend my weeks and years one day.

I've blocked out every Monday as my creative day where I spend time thinking and working on new creative ideas. From Tuesday through to Thursday, I work normal office hours and organise most of my meetings during this time.

On Fridays I attend my children's school assembly first thing in the morning – they won't be young forever and I cherish making the most of this opportunity for a glimpse into their school life. Then I visit a new café or one of my old favourites to work remotely. I love food and I love being in inspiring cafés, so I look forward to this change of workplace on Fridays, out of the office, reflecting on the week (what can I do better?) and planning for the following week. I also usually build in a work-related meeting – specifically for inspiration or relationship-building rather than anything of day-to-day urgency. This could be someone that I have on my list of 101 people to meet, or a friend or a colleague I want to catch up with. I love Fridays – they combine all my favourite things: family, reflecting, planning and being inspired. And I end the working week with making healthy pizzas with the children on Friday nights. They call it 'Pizza Friday'!

Having worked seven days a week for many years to build my business, I love now being flexible about where I work and how I spread my many working hours across the week. It's a dream for me. I know many people don't have that choice, but if that's something you would love, why not add that to your 101 Dreams List and, over time, find a way to make it happen?

---

19 TIMOTHY FERRISS, *THE 4-HOUR WORK WEEK* (NEW YORK: HARMONY BOOKS, 2007)

That's an insight into my dream week. It doesn't always look like that, but it often does. Progress, not perfection.

To get to my dream week took a few years. I broke that larger dream down into smaller goals and started taking steps towards it one by one – changing my schedule and availability, blocking out time and setting new habits to support the dream. I started by blocking out ninety minutes a day from 9am to 10:30am to work on my most important projects without any interruption. This made a massive difference to my productivity, freeing up time elsewhere. Maybe you could start with that?

It worked for me, and so I encourage you to think about what your dream week would look like and start setting goals to work towards it. As my lovely colleague, Neil, once said, 'We all have to do things we don't enjoy in our roles.' I agree with that, but I think we can all work towards doing less of the things we don't enjoy. Who knows, by learning and growing in different ways, you may start to appreciate those tricky areas too!

I'd love you to think about what a dream week looks like for you, day by day.

When I dream about my dream day, I always start with Sunday, as it's my favourite, but I want you to choose whatever day you love most. Maybe you love Fridays because it's nearly the weekend. Maybe you love Mondays because you love the work you get to do.

In the following exercises, you'll get to choose whatever is your favourite and dream up your dream day. Then you'll do the same for your dream week and again for your dream year.

Work out what the answers look like for you, so you can understand what it could feel like, and how to work towards it, step by step, to edge closer to what you define as your dream life.

I do these exercises every year in January so I can work towards embracing a dream week every week in that year.

EXERCISE

IN YOUR DREAM LIFE JOURNAL:

01 /

CHOOSE YOUR FAVOURITE DAY OF THE WEEK. IF THAT DAY WERE A DREAM DAY, WHAT WOULD IT LOOK LIKE? WHAT WOULD IT INVOLVE? HOW WOULD IT FEEL AT THE START AND THE END OF EACH DAY? HOW WOULD IT FEEL DURING THE DAY? WRITE DETAILED ANSWERS FOR EACH DAY OF THE WEEK.

+ DON'T PLACE ANY CONSTRAINTS ON YOURSELF. JUST DREAM. THERE'LL BE TIME LATER TO SEE HOW THIS FITS INTO YOUR REAL LIFE.

YOUR DREAM DAY

+ WHAT WOULD IT INVOLVE?
+ WOULD YOU SPEND IT ON YOUR OWN, OR WITH FAMILY OR FRIENDS?
+ WHAT WOULD YOU LOVE TO DO?
+ WHAT WOULD YOU EAT?
+ WHERE WOULD YOU GO?
+ WHAT WOULD MAKE IT TRULY PERFECT?
+ HOW WILL YOU FEEL AT THE START OF IT AND AT THE END OF IT?

+ WHEN YOU'RE SATISFIED IT'S RIGHT FOR YOU, THINK ABOUT HOW YOU COULD MAKE THAT DREAM DAY A REGULAR REALITY:
    + WHAT DO YOU NEED TO DO TO WELCOME MORE OF THAT DREAM DAY INTO YOUR LIFE?
    + WHAT DO YOU NEED TO STOP DOING?

---

02 /

ONCE YOU'VE DONE ONE DAY, YOU CAN START TO THINK ABOUT WHAT YOUR DREAM WEEK WOULD LOOK LIKE. WHAT DO YOU DO EVERY DAY OVER A WEEK? WHAT DO YOU MAKE TIME FOR? WHAT DO YOU NOT MAKE TIME FOR? WRITE IT DOWN IN DETAIL.

YOUR DREAM WEEK

+ HOW MUCH WOULD YOU WORK?
+ HOW OFTEN WOULD YOU TRAVEL?
+ WHAT WOULD YOU DO ON YOUR WEEKENDS?
+ HOW MUCH TIME WOULD YOU DEDICATE TO CREATIVITY AND INSPIRATION, OR LEARNING AND EDUCATION?

EXERCISE

03 /

NOW LET'S PAINT A PICTURE OF YOUR DREAM YEAR, BY MONTH, IN THE TABLE ON THE FOLLOWING SPREAD OR IN YOUR DREAM LIFE JOURNAL. THIS DRAFT OF YOUR DREAM YEAR WILL CHANGE OVER THE COURSE OF YOUR LIFE, BUT TODAY WE'RE FOCUSED ON YOUR DREAM YEAR AS YOU SEE IT FROM YOUR PERSPECTIVE RIGHT NOW.

+ CHOOSE YOUR FAVOURITE MONTH OF THE YEAR. IF THAT MONTH WERE A DREAM MONTH, WHAT WOULD IT LOOK LIKE? WHAT WOULD IT INVOLVE? HOW WOULD IT FEEL AT THE START AND THE END OF THE MONTH? HOW WOULD IT FEEL DURING THE MONTH?
+ REPEAT FOR EACH MONTH.
+ WHEN DO YOU TAKE HOLIDAYS? WHEN ARE THE SIGNIFICANT CELEBRATIONS? WHEN IS THE BEST TIME OF YEAR FOR YOU TO REFLECT AND PLAN FOR THE YEAR AHEAD? WHERE DOES WORK OR STUDY FIT? WHAT WILL YOU MAKE TIME FOR THAT YOU'RE NOT MAKING TIME FOR NOW? WRITE IT ALL DOWN.

---

04 /

NOW THAT YOU'VE DESIGNED YOUR DREAM DAYS, WEEK AND YEAR, THINK DEEPLY ABOUT THE FOLLOWING QUESTIONS AND WRITE DOWN YOUR THOUGHTS:

+ HOW CAN YOU WELCOME MORE OF YOUR DREAM DAYS, WEEKS AND YEARS INTO YOUR LIFE?
+ WHAT ARE THREE ACTIONS YOU CAN TAKE TODAY TO MAKE THE DAYS, WEEKS AND YEARS AHEAD SOMETHING CLOSER TO YOUR DREAM DAYS, WEEKS AND YEARS?
+ IF ANY SIGNIFICANT DREAMS HAVE COME OUT OF THIS EXERCISE FOR YOU, TAKE SOME TIME TO ADD THEM TO YOUR 101 DREAMS LIST, WHICH YOU'LL REFER BACK TO LATER IN OUR JOURNEY TOGETHER.

YOUR DREAM YEAR

JANUARY	FEBRUARY

MARCH	APRIL

MAY	JUNE

YOUR DREAM YEAR

JULY	AUGUST

SEPTEMBER	OCTOBER

NOVEMBER	DECEMBER

1

EXPLORE WHAT A DREAM DAY,
WEEK AND YEAR LOOKS LIKE FOR
YOU, AND THEN START WORKING
TOWARDS MAKING THAT
YOUR REALITY

2

TAKE ACTION IN SMALL WAYS
TO BEGIN TO INTRODUCE MORE
FROM YOUR DREAM DAY, WEEK
AND YEAR INTO YOUR
EVERYDAY LIFE

3

ENJOY THE JOURNEY,
AND NEVER LOSE SIGHT
OF YOUR END GOAL

12

START PULLING IT TOGETHER –
YOUR DREAM LIFE LOOKS LIKE THIS...

YOUR DREAM LIFE STARTS HERE

I'm so excited for this chapter because we're going to start getting specific and bringing together everything we've learnt to start building a more structured vision for your dream life.

As you've seen, there are so many different ways to practise looking at and exploring your dreams. As we explored earlier, I like to start by making a list of all my dreams straight from the heart and without constraint, and then adding to it in various ways.

But right now is where we will really start to make progress – focusing on your dreams for specific life areas. For example, think about everything you dream of for your career. Then think of everything you dream of for your family. Breaking down your life into areas like this will really help you develop a clearer picture of the life you want to live – your dream life. Exciting!

Most importantly, I want to remind you not to question your dreams.

If they matter to you, that's all you need to think about right now. Don't worry about how realistic they are or how hard it might be to make them happen. Forget all of that. Park it, and we'll get to that later.

Remember in the exercises ahead to dream as if you have all the money, time and resources you need, and – no matter what you do – you can't fail.

If you ever get a little stuck while dreaming, there's a great book called *The Magic of Thinking Big* by David Schwartz[20] that I highly recommend. When I read this book – and I've read it so many times – I always feel encouraged to dream even bigger. It may be a little old-fashioned nowadays, but it's still very inspiring.

---

20 DAVID SCHWARTZ, *THE MAGIC OF THINKING BIG* (NEW JERSEY: PRENTICE HALL, 1959)

So, onto the exercises. I've included below a list of the life areas that I focus on at this point in the process. I hope these are general enough to fit your circumstances too, but you can choose whatever areas feel right for you. Make sure you add your values to the list too, but don't double up if they're covered by the list already. Similarly, add any major passions or anything that came out of your work on your purpose (again, only if they're not already covered).

LIFE AREAS I DREAM UNDER...

+ CAREER AND FINANCES (THIS ONE COVERS MY 'KIKKI.K' VALUE, A PASSION AND MY PURPOSE FOR 'CREATING AND SHARING BEAUTIFUL AND MEANINGFUL THINGS')
+ EDUCATION AND LEARNING (THIS ONE COVERS MY 'PERSONAL DEVELOPMENT' VALUE)
+ HEALTH, WELLNESS AND FITNESS (THIS ONE COVERS MY 'HEALTH AND WELLNESS' VALUE)
+ FAMILY AND RELATIONSHIPS (THIS ONE COVERS MY 'FAMILY' VALUE AND PURPOSE)
+ HOME (THIS ONE COVERS MY 'HOME' VALUE AND FAMILY PURPOSE)
+ SPIRITUALITY AND SENSE OF PURPOSE
+ TRAVEL AND EXPERIENCES (THIS ONE COVERS MY 'TRAVEL' VALUE)
+ HOBBIES/FUN
+ COMMUNITY AND ENVIRONMENT (THIS ONE COVERS MY 'SHARING, INSPIRING AND EMPOWERING OTHERS' VALUE AND MY 'HELP THE WORLD TO DREAM' PURPOSE)
+ THINGS I ASPIRE TO HAVE IN MY LIFE

The reason why this kind of dreaming is so powerful is because our lives are made up of so many different elements. Sometimes when we dream in big general terms, we overlook some of the things we've decided are important to us.

It doesn't matter how you divide up your life or the names you give to each area as long as it feels right for you. Use the above list as a guide and tweak it as necessary to fit your life.

What matters is making time to dream in each key area of your own life, and finding inspiration in the process. If you're unsure, look hard at your lists of values, passions and purpose. In these, you will find guidance to the areas of your life that matter most.

When I'm doing this kind of dreaming, I start by picking just one area and reflecting on where I'm at now, where I've been and where I want to go. I visualise that life area as if my dreams have come true so I can see it clearly in my mind. What would that life area feel like and look like if it were perfect for me?

Then I let my thoughts run wild and write down all the big and little dreams I have for that specific area. I usually replicate some of the dreams on my 101 Dreams List as I do this, as I find the repetition really valuable and can always edit out the double-ups later.

While I'm doing this, if I think of another dream for another area (which can easily happen when you're in dreaming mode), I make a note of it somewhere else, then bring my focus back to the area I'm working on and continue.

I start with a blank page, and when I'm done I go through my 101 Dreams List and add anything from that to the relevant area. This new set of pages then becomes my Dream Life Blueprint and it's the main place I focus on as I move on from here with my dreaming practice.

There's no right or wrong way to do this, but for each area – one area at a time – ask yourself the same questions again that you asked yourself in chapter 1, including:

+ *What would you do if you knew you could not fail?*
+ *What would you do with your life if you had all the time and money you needed?*

I've created a guided visualisation you can access online to help you with this process. So if you'd like to hear the questions asked as you just focus on visualising and writing your thoughts down, go to www.kikki-k.com/bookresources.

EXERCISE

Think about how you want to feel in each area and what helps you feel that way. And above all, think big!

IN YOUR DREAM LIFE JOURNAL:

01 /

MAKE A LIST OF THE LIFE AREAS THAT MAKE SENSE FOR YOU (IT CAN HELP TO LOOK BACK AT YOUR LISTS OF PASSIONS, VALUES AND PURPOSE), OR USE MY LIFE AREAS LISTED ON THE PREVIOUS PAGES FOR INSPIRATION.

02 /

DEDICATE A PAGE IN YOUR DREAM LIFE JOURNAL TO EACH LIFE AREA. THIS WILL BECOME YOUR DREAM LIFE BLUEPRINT.

03 /

THEN, ONE BY ONE, VISUALISE EACH OF YOUR LIFE AREAS AS IF YOUR DREAMS HAVE COME TRUE. WHAT DOES IT FEEL LIKE? WHAT DOES IT LOOK LIKE?

LET YOUR IMAGINATION RUN WILD AND WRITE DOWN ALL YOUR AMAZING, BIG PICTURE DREAMS FOR THAT LIFE AREA. DON'T OVERTHINK IT. JUST DREAM LIKE YOU DID AT THE START OF THIS BOOK, FOCUSING ON THE TWO KEY QUESTIONS ON THE PREVIOUS PAGE, AS YOU CONTEMPLATE EACH LIFE AREA. WHAT WOULD YOU DO IN THAT AREA OF YOUR LIFE IF YOU KNEW YOU COULD NOT FAIL? WHAT WOULD YOU DO IN THAT AREA OF YOUR LIFE IF YOU HAD ALL THE TIME AND MONEY YOU NEEDED?

DON'T WORRY TOO MUCH ABOUT TIMEFRAMES OR OTHER LIMITATIONS. JUST DUMP YOUR IDEAS.

04 /

NOW GO BACK TO YOUR 101 DREAMS LIST AND REWRITE THE DREAMS THAT ARE MOST RELEVANT FOR EACH LIFE AREA ON THE PAGE CORRESPONDING TO THAT LIFE AREA. WHAT YOU'VE CREATED IS YOUR DREAM LIFE BLUEPRINT.

START PULLING IT TOGETHER -
YOUR DREAM LIFE LOOKS LIKE THIS...

1 YOUR LIFE CAN BE DIVIDED UP INTO DIFFERENT AREAS THAT ALL INFLUENCE ONE ANOTHER AND CONTRIBUTE TOWARDS YOUR OVERALL FEELING OF JOY, MEANING, PURPOSE AND INSPIRATION

2 MAKE TIME TO DREAM IN EACH KEY AREA OF YOUR OWN LIFE

3 DON'T QUESTION YOUR DREAMS - IF THEY MATTER TO YOU, THAT'S ALL THAT MATTERS

THE MORE CLOSELY YOU GET IN TOUCH

WITH YOUR DREAMS, THE MORE ABLE

YOU ARE TO MAKE THEM REAL. THE

MORE VIVIDLY YOU CONSIDER HOW YOU

WANT YOUR WORLD TO BE, THE MORE

REAL AND EFFECTIVE TOOLS YOU WILL

HAVE FOR MAKING IT SO.

- RALPH MARSTON -

13

VISUALISE – WRITE YOUR DREAM LIFE STORY

YOUR DREAM LIFE STARTS HERE

There's something so powerful about visualisation. As a child, my love for design started early. I loved visiting people's homes and being inspired by the interiors, art and design. Even at an early age, I visualised my dream home (and dream wardrobe!)

Visualisation is a proven means of transporting yourself out of your here-and-now thinking. It helps you activate your creativity and tap into the power of your subconscious mind to vividly imagine the future.

In my experience, when you visualise your dreams, you're more likely to achieve them. Because when you can see and feel something, you believe in it too. And once you have that image in your mind, you start to subconsciously and consciously do everything you can to make it happen.

As an example, home is really important to me and I'm always visualising my dream house. Years ago, I came across a place while I was out walking that I really wanted to live in. I even started calling it 'our dream house'. It wasn't up for sale or for lease, but I kept walking past it anyway, almost daily for about six months, visualising myself living there. I even put a picture of it on my Vision Board (you'll read more about this in chapter 15). The vision of living in that particular home really inspired me and led me to start looking through property sites online, something I wouldn't have thought of earlier.

One day, our dream home came up for rent and I happened to stumble across the listing as I was browsing a website. I applied and we moved in. Visualising myself living there had inspired my actions that led to that dream coming true for my family and me.

I truly believe you have a better chance of making things happen if you create and keep in your mind a clear vision of yourself achieving your dreams.

Placing images of those dreams where you'll see them daily certainly helps. This means you'll notice opportunities when they arise instead of missing them because you're distracted or too busy doing other things.

While writing this book, I kept visualising the book cover. I had one of our lovely designers create a rough concept for the cover and I put it on my fridge. Something really shifted for me when I saw the cover printed. It felt so real. I could feel the finished book in my hands and imagine it in the hands of millions of readers like you. I imagined the book in my favourite bookstores and I visualised it on bestseller lists because I want to share the power of dreaming far and wide.

Will that happen? I don't know. But I do know that if I keep visualising it, it will inspire me to do the best I can to add value to this book and to achieve my dream of inspiring millions of people to discover the transformational power of dreaming.

Before jumping into this exciting exercise, let's first reflect quickly on where we are in this process of creating your dream life...

You've opened the door and started to dream from your heart and without constraints. You've started to organise those dreams by life areas that mean something to you. You've explored your passions, your values, your purpose. You've thought about what you don't want to regret. You've been inspired by the dreams of others and you know you're in the driver's seat of your own life. You've thought about how your dream week and dream year could look. A real picture is starting to form in your mind as you're imagining how your dream life could unfold.

Now it's time for some fun. We're going to do what many elite athletes do as they prepare themselves for competition. It's time to transport yourself into your future – time to use the power of your imagination to visualise in rich detail your life five years from now – and then to put down in writing the story of your future dream life.

I love doing this exercise. It's a process I've done so many times over the years, and I suggest you do it at least annually. Every time I do it I get something amazing from it.

It's such a useful way to rise above the busyness of everyday life and free yourself to imagine in crystal-clear detail what life could look like for you, and your loved ones, five years in the future.

You have to really embrace it. Tap your creativity to create vivid pictures of your future in your mind's eye. Let go of thinking too rationally – really challenge yourself to do that – and just have fun with the exercise as visions spring into your mind and flow onto paper, for you to sift through and be inspired by later.

I love to work five years out because it's far enough into the future to take you away from your here and now, but not too far so as to be unrealistic and remote. And trust me, you can get a LOT done in those five years.

I've created another guided visualisation you can access online to help you with this particular process. So if you'd like to hear the questions asked as you just focus on visualising and writing your thoughts down, go to www.kikki-k.com/bookresources.

So, get yourself into your inspiring space and state of mind and, in your Dream Life Journal, I want you to start by writing down today's exact date and time, but change the year to be five years from today.

EXERCISE

IN YOUR DREAM LIFE JOURNAL:

01 /

IN YOUR MIND, TAKE A LEAP AND MENTALLY TRANSPORT YOURSELF TO THAT EXACT DAY AND TIME IN YOUR FUTURE.

USING PRESENT TENSE, WRITE DOWN HOW OLD YOU ARE ON THIS DAY, AND USE YOUR IMAGINATION TO VISUALISE THAT IT IS THIS DATE. YOU ARE THAT AGE.

'IT'S _____ AND I'M _____ YEARS OLD.'

STOP TO IMAGINE THAT. BREATHE AND RELAX INTO HOW THAT FEELS.

USE YOUR IMAGINATION TO DESCRIBE – IN WRITING – HOW YOU WANT TO LOOK AND FEEL ON THAT DAY IN YOUR FUTURE.

WRITE WHATEVER COMES TO MIND ... SHORT AND SIMPLE. BULLET POINTS ARE FINE.

STOP AND THINK ABOUT THE AGES OF OTHER SIGNIFICANT PEOPLE IN YOUR LIFE. WRITE THEIR NAMES AND AGES DOWN. THIS CAN REALLY HELP TRANSPORT YOU MENTALLY TO THAT DAY IN YOUR FUTURE. DESCRIBE BRIEFLY IN WRITING HOW THEY LOOK TOO...

---

02 /

NOW LET'S MOVE TO EACH OF YOUR KEY LIFE AREAS THAT YOU IDENTIFIED IN THE PREVIOUS CHAPTER. ONE BY ONE, IMAGINE HOW THAT AREA OF YOUR LIFE LOOKS FOR YOU AS YOU REFLECT ON IT ON THIS DAY IN YOUR FUTURE.

AS YOU WORK THROUGH EACH LIFE AREA, USE THE FOLLOWING PROMPTS TO DESCRIBE WHAT YOU SEE AND FEEL WHEN YOU LOOK AROUND AT THAT ELEMENT OF YOUR FUTURE STORY.

IN THIS LIFE AREA:

+ THE THINGS I FEEL PROUD OF INCLUDE...
+ MY BEST FRIENDS TELL ME...
+ THE THINGS I LOVE MOST ARE...
+ WHEN I LOOK AT MYSELF IN THE MIRROR AND THINK ABOUT HOW I'M GOING
  IN THIS LIFE AREA I FEEL...
+ THE THINGS I SEE AROUND ME ARE...
+ ON A WEEKLY BASIS I...

EXERCISE

03 /

AS YOU DO THIS EXERCISE, TRY COMPARING - IN EACH LIFE AREA - HOW YOUR LIFE LOOKS AND FEELS TO YOU AT THAT POINT IN YOUR FUTURE, RELATIVE TO THE LIFE THAT YOU'RE LIVING NOW.

+ DESCRIBE THE DIFFERENCES AND HOW YOU FEEL ABOUT THEM.
+ WHAT IS BETTER ABOUT YOUR LIFE ON THIS DAY FIVE YEARS INTO THE FUTURE?
+ HOW HAVE YOU MADE PROGRESS?
+ WHAT ARE YOU WORKING ON?
+ WHO ARE YOU SPENDING TIME WITH? HOW DOES THAT FEEL?
+ WHAT HAVE YOU LET GO OF? WHAT HAVE YOU EMBRACED?

AS YOU WRITE - REMEMBER, SHORT BULLET POINTS ARE JUST FINE - TRY TO USE WORDS THAT ARE COLOURFUL, STIMULATING, EVOCATIVE AND GENUINE. KEEP IT SIMPLE, BUT THE CLEARER THE PICTURE YOU CAN CREATE FOR YOURSELF, THE BETTER.

---

04 /

WHEN YOU'RE DONE, COME BACK OVER THE NEXT FEW DAYS TO READ OVER WHAT YOU'VE WRITTEN. ADD TO IT. ADJUST IT. AND MAKE IT AUTHENTICALLY YOURS. THIS IS SUCH AN EXCITING STEP YOU'RE TAKING.

THIS PICTURE OF YOUR DREAM LIFE - YOUR DREAM LIFE STORY - IS YOUR DESTINATION, AND EVERY CHAPTER FROM THIS POINT FORWARD WILL HELP YOU CREATE A ROADMAP TO REACH IT. WHENEVER YOU FEEL A LITTLE LOST, RETURN TO THAT IMAGE AND REMIND YOURSELF OF WHAT YOU'RE WORKING TOWARDS AND HOW IT'S GOING TO FEEL WHEN YOU ARRIVE AT THAT DAY, FIVE YEARS FROM NOW.

REVISIT AND REWRITE YOUR DREAM LIFE STORY OVER TIME. REFLECT ON IT OFTEN. IMAGINE IT IN VIVID DETAIL. THE MORE YOU VISUALISE IT, THE CLEARER AND MORE FOCUSED YOU'LL BECOME ON MAKING IT HAPPEN AND THE MORE YOUR SUBCONSCIOUS MIND WILL FILTER OUT WHAT YOU DON'T NEED AND FILTER IN WHAT YOU DO.

YOU WILL START TO ATTRACT WONDERFUL AND EXCITING OPPORTUNITIES THAT WILL TAKE YOU STEP BY STEP TOWARDS YOUR DREAM LIFE.

ADD ANYTHING NEW THAT COMES FROM THIS EXERCISE TO YOUR DREAM LIFE BLUEPRINT AND VISION BOARD (WE WILL LOOK AT THIS IN MORE DETAIL IN CHAPTER 15).

VISUALISE - WRITE YOUR DREAM LIFE STORY

1 VISUALISATION IS A POWERFUL TOOL TO HELP YOU ACHIEVE YOUR DREAMS

2 USE THE POWER OF YOUR IMAGINATION TO VISUALISE IN RICH DETAIL YOUR LIFE FIVE YEARS FROM NOW

3 WRITING YOUR DREAM LIFE STORY WILL HELP YOU ATTRACT EXCITING AND WONDERFUL OPPORTUNITIES THAT WILL TAKE YOU STEP BY STEP CLOSER TO YOUR DREAM LIFE

4 KEEP THIS STORY OF YOUR DREAM LIFE NEARBY AND IN YOUR MIND

'OBSTACLES WILL COME,
BUT IF YOUR DREAM IS STRONG...'

OPRAH WINFREY

Oprah Winfrey's story is amazing and such a brilliant example of the power of dreaming no matter where you start out in life – and her start was a particularly challenging one.

Known around the world as a media personality, actress, producer and philanthropist, she's probably best known for her talk show *The Oprah Winfrey Show,* which was the highest-rated television program of its kind in history.

The things I find amazing about Oprah's story, which many people may not know, is that she came from such a humble background and overcame so many obstacles to achieve her dreams and do the most inspiring work to help others – including people like Dr Tererai Trent. I'm so grateful Oprah gave me permission to share this story with you.

Born into poverty in rural Mississippi to a teenage single mother and later raised in a rough inner-city neighbourhood, Oprah faced challenges during her childhood and early teens that you'd wish on no one. But while she was still in high school, she landed a job in radio and began co-anchoring the local evening news at the age of nineteen.

It was the start of an incredible career that saw her being awarded the United States' highest civilian honour – the Presidential Medal of Freedom – by President Barack Obama in 2013. During the presentation ceremony, her story was well described as follows:

'In 1986, there were few women – and even fewer women of color – with a national platform to discuss the issues and events shaping our times. But over the 25 years that followed, Oprah's innate gift for tapping into our most fervent hopes and deepest fears drew millions of viewers across every background, making her show the highest-rated talk show in television history.'[21]

An amazing achievement considering where she started from and the barriers she faced.

---

21 'OBAMA SPEAKS AT PRESIDENTIAL MEDAL OF FREEDOM CEREMONY (TRANSCRIPT, VIDEO)', POLITICO, NOVEMBER 20, 2013, HTTPS://WWW.POLITICO.COM/STORY/2013/11/PRESIDENT-OBAMA-PRESIDENTIAL-MEDAL-OF-FREEDOM-CEREMONY-TRANSCRIPT-VIDEO-100140

'Off screen [she] has used her influence to support underserviced communities and to lift up the lives of young people – especially young women – around the world. In [Oprah's] story we are reminded that no dream can be deferred when we refuse to let life's obstacles keep us down.'[22]

Below is a story of Oprah's from when she was about four or five years old. It shows the power of dreams and self-belief, and sends shivers down my spine.

'My grandmother was a maid – that's all she ever knew. The only real expectation she held for me was that I would one day become a maid and in her words, "have some good white folks", meaning people who would not speak negatively about me, who would allow me to take food home, who would be good to me, would treat me with some level of dignity and respect. That was my grandmother's dream for me, but I had another dream for myself – more than a dream, I had a belief for myself.

And I remember watching her hang up clothes on a line one day and say to me, "You have to watch me … because one day you'll have to do this" … and knowing inside myself that that was not going to be my life… Because I sensed that and was connected to that … I knew that would not be my life. I knew that I will not be hanging clothes on a line in a backyard in Mississippi … and that belief that that would not be my life is what I held onto for the longest of times…

I just, no matter what, believed that there was something bigger, greater, more for me. I had no idea that it would take the form that it has taken – that I would become a person on television and that I would do all the things that I've done… I just believed that there was something more and I was always cognisant of what that more was.'[23]

This story also shows how powerful it can be to know and visualise what things you *don't want to do* – and how valuable that can be as a catalyst to motivate you to find your purpose and follow your passions. So, no matter where you're starting from, remember and be inspired by the fact that there are many people who have come from less privileged situations than yours and have still found a way to bring their dreams to life.

Let Oprah's story inspire you to dream big, no matter where you're starting in life. Take some time now while it's fresh in your mind to ponder on it and, in the space on the opposite page, or in your Dream Life Journal, write down anything you've learnt that you could apply in your own life.

---

22 IBID.
23 'OPRAH'S BELIEF IN HERSELF', YOUTUBE VIDEO, 3:01, POSTED BY THE 'OPRAH WINFREY NETWORK', OCTOBER 13, 2011, HTTPS://WWW.YOUTUBE.COM/WATCH?V=G1MPB5SJAEU.

LIFE DOESN'T HAVE TO BE PERFECT

TO BE WONDERFUL.

- ANNETTE FUNICELLO -

14

PRIORITISE YOUR DREAMS

YOUR DREAM LIFE STARTS HERE

Isn't it just the most exciting to dream without limits? I love it, and I know that you're now finding the magic in it too. The practice of dreaming is powerful, but what's even more powerful is taking the action required to make those dreams a reality.

Now that you've worked through the previous dreaming exercises – which have all been leading you to this exciting point – it's time to choose what is most important for you to work on first, and what can wait a little or wait indefinitely.

As I said, you can do anything, but you can't do everything at once. You'll have to park some dreams for now, and that is perfectly okay. So what are the dreams that, deep down, feel most meaningful for you to make a start on? Which of them give you butterflies when you say them out loud?

Do you dream about starting your own business, changing your career or making your current role even more amazing? Or do you dream about buying a new home, making a trip happen, or being as fit and healthy as you can so you can make your dreams come true over a long life?

Your dreams can be big or small. One of my big dreams is to create our dream home. The house I want and can't afford yet. But just because we can't afford it yet, doesn't stop me dreaming about it.

Whatever you choose, make sure that they're the dreams that are most meaningful to you. Don't choose ones you think you *should* care about – remember, you are in the driver's seat.

I remember a friend of mine telling me they had been inspired by another person's dream to 'find a valuable artefact on an archaeological dig'. My friend added it to his 101 Dreams List, only to realise later that wasn't a dream that really meant anything to him at all. He'd just got caught up in the romantic idea of doing that, and decided later it wasn't meaningful to him.

Another example someone recently shared with me was that she'd pursued an education and career in law – on reflection, because that was a dream of her parents. After a few years in law, she finally decided it wasn't for her and she dreamed of doing something creative. I hear this one so regularly. Law was an obvious education choice initially because she was good at school, but it wasn't her dream.

Every year I choose my top three dreams to focus on for the year. Then I set actions against each for me to carry out. That's what you're going to do at the end of this chapter.

So how do you pick just three dreams, if you have hundreds of dreams and want to do it all? This requires some thinking and some prioritising.

I think we all know deep inside what we most want in life – we just don't take the time to work out where to start. But by writing your dreams down, reading over them and rewriting them in whatever timeframe you think works for you, your priorities will become clearer. I often find that health dreams are great to start with because, as your health improves, you will have more energy for chasing your other dreams.

Sharing your dreams with others in your life is another way to help you prioritise them. When our children were very young, I'd added a dream to my 101 Dreams List that one day I wanted us to be able to take the family back to my hometown in Sweden to live for a year. I wanted to give them a taste of my own childhood, close to their Swedish family, where they could experience all things Swedish firsthand. I read and re-read that dream many times over the years. I then discussed it with Paul, Ax and Tiff too, and we decided that we wanted to make it happen while the children were still in primary school. But with a very busy working life, I struggled to see exactly when we could fit it in and I wasn't ready to take that decision about when to make the dream a priority.

I just wasn't mentally prepared and, initially, I wasn't sure I could do my role properly while living away from my team for a year. Being a very visual person – and a person whose style is strongly collaborative – working alongside my Melbourne-based team was important to me. I was worried I might miss too many important meetings and conversations.

But because the whole family shared the dream, it was brought up many times during our dinner conversations, as was the question of when was the right time to make it happen.

In the end, we listed the pros and cons, and voted as a family – with Axel at eight years of age and Tiffany at five given equal votes as Paul and me. Everyone except me voted to do it the following year, and in our home 'a vote is a vote', so I had to make it happen.

I'm so glad I did. It forced me to prioritise that dream and to find a way to make it happen that would be good for the business too. I got to spend priceless time with my family and friends and take endless walks in the beautiful Swedish nature that triggered many great ideas. The children were able to experience all the Swedish traditions and loved school in Sweden.

As it happened, the timing also lined up perfectly with us opening kikki.K stores in London, and with Sweden so close to London, it made my work easier for that time. In the end it turned out to be perfect timing. If I hadn't shared that dream with my family – and involved them in prioritising it – I may have put it off for much longer, and maybe the dream wouldn't have come true. So, consider involving your family or significant others in helping you prioritise your big dreams.

So, at the end of this chapter, I'd love for you to choose just three dreams from all the dreams on your Dream Life Blueprint. Pick the dreams that are the most meaningful to you. The dreams that will have the biggest impact on you living your dream life. The dreams that make your heart beat a little faster... Write them down in your Dream Life Journal as the three you're going to focus on.

Once you've chosen those, it's time to get clear on your 'Why?' for each. The process of asking yourself 'Why?' – why you want it to be a priority, why you want to achieve it, why it's important to you – is one of the most important and useful exercises for you right now.

So, looking back at your three dreams, why are they each important to you? Do they reflect your passions, purpose and values?

The point of this exercise is to make sure that your dreams are really your dreams and that you really have a burning reason to make them happen. A real hunger that will drive you to do whatever it takes, and which will make it easy for you to say no to other things so you can focus on achieving your dreams. We live in a world where so many things influence us. This is unavoidable and not always a bad thing, but when it comes to dreaming, you want your dreams to be authentically yours. Your dreams should reflect you and your values, and mean something deeply important to you so that they pull you towards your dream life – not someone else's idea of a dream life.

Once you're clear on those top three dreams and why they're the most meaningful for you at this point in time, the next step will be to take action and set yourself up for success with the approach that we'll start to explore in the next chapter. But first...

YOU CAN DO ANYTHING, BUT NOT

EVERYTHING ALL AT ONCE.

- ANON. -

EXERCISE

IN YOUR DREAM LIFE JOURNAL (OR THE SPACE BELOW):

01/

WHAT ARE THE THREE DREAMS THAT ARE MOST MEANINGFUL TO YOU?

02/

WHY ARE THESE DREAMS IMPORTANT TO YOU? WHAT ARE YOUR BURNING REASONS
TO MAKE THEM HAPPEN?

03/

WHY DO YOU WANT TO GET STARTED ON THESE DREAMS FIRST?
ON THE OPPOSITE PAGE IS AN EXAMPLE OF MY TOP THREE PRIORITY DREAMS SO YOU
CAN SEE HOW IT WORKS.

DREAM	WHY THIS DREAM?	WHY THIS DREAM FIRST?

EXERCISE

DREAM	WHY THIS DREAM?	WHY THIS DREAM FIRST?
1. TO BE THE FITTEST I HAVE EVER BEEN	BEING FITTER WILL HELP ME FEEL GREAT, HAVE MORE ENERGY TO MAKE MORE DREAMS COME TRUE – AND THE REGULAR EXERCISE WILL HELP ME SLEEP BETTER. ALSO SUPPORTS MY OTHER DREAM TO LIVE TO 120 YEARS OF AGE!	THIS WILL HAVE A POSITIVE IMPACT ON LOTS OF MY OTHER LIFE AREAS AND DREAMS. IF I'M FITTER AND HEALTHIER, I WILL HAVE MORE ENERGY TO GET TO MY OTHER DREAMS QUICKER AND MAKE MORE DREAMS COME TRUE IN MY LIFETIME.
2. TO WRITE A BESTSELLING BOOK TO INSPIRE AND EMPOWER PEOPLE TO DREAM	I KNOW THE INCREDIBLE IMPACT OF DREAMING FROM PERSONAL EXPERIENCE, AND I KNOW THERE ARE SO MANY PEOPLE WHO WILL BENEFIT. A BOOK CAN REACH SO MANY, AND SUPPORTS MY DREAM TO INSPIRE 101 MILLION PEOPLE ACROSS THE WORLD TO WRITE DOWN THREE DREAMS AND MAKE THEM HAPPEN.	BEING FORTUNATE TO HAVE WORKED OUT MY OWN SIMPLE APPROACH TO DREAMING AND DOING, I WANT TO HELP OTHER PEOPLE DO THE SAME, AND MY DREAM TO REACH 101 MILLION PEOPLE WILL TAKE SOME TIME SO I NEED TO MAKE IT HAPPEN NOW.
3. BEING PRESENT WITH THE CHILDREN EVERY DAY AFTER SCHOOL	BECAUSE OUR CHILDREN ARE GROWING UP SO FAST AND I REALLY WANT TO MAKE THE MOST OF THIS TIME TOGETHER. I KNOW BY BEING PRESENT WITH THEM, I WILL ALSO BE ABLE TO BE MORE PRESENT IN MY OTHER AREAS OF LIFE.	LIFE IS SHORT AND OUR CHILDREN WILL ONLY BE YOUNG FOR A SHORT TIME. I DON'T WANT TO REGRET NOT SPENDING ENOUGH TIME WITH THEM.

PRIORITISE YOUR DREAMS

1 YOU CAN DO ANYTHING, BUT NOT EVERYTHING AT ONCE

2 PRIORITISING YOUR THREE MOST IMPORTANT AND MEANINGFUL DREAMS WILL SPUR YOU TO ACTION AND SET YOU UP FOR SUCCESS

3 MAKE SURE THAT THE DREAMS YOU CHOOSE TO PRIORITISE ARE AUTHENTIC TO YOU AND REFLECT YOUR PASSIONS AND VALUES

15

LOOK AT YOUR DREAMS DAILY

YOUR DREAM LIFE STARTS HERE

I love how everyone gets excited about a new year, me included. Nearly all of us set New Year's resolutions, yet few stick to them. And I believe there's a very good reason for this. Few people write their resolutions down on paper, and few of the ones who *do* write them down look at them every day.

I believe the key to committing to and achieving your dreams is to look at them daily. I create vision boards every year with all my dreams on them so that I see them every day and am reminded of what I'm working towards.

First, I write my dreams on my Vision Board. I also add pictures, words and quotes that remind me of how it will feel to achieve my dreams and inspire me to do what I need to do to make the dreams real. It's so powerful – you have to try it.

If you've never created a vision board, now's the time. Creating a visual representation of your dreams, especially the top three dreams you've just identified, is a beautiful and powerful way to help support you to turn them into reality. A vision board acts as a tool that helps motivate you to take action to make your dreams come true. Not only is it fun to make, it's something you can easily look at across the course of the day to remind yourself of the journey you're on.

Depending on what your dreams are, you might have images that represent travel destinations you want to visit, or images that reflect the sense of joy or peace you strive for each day. You might have pictures that represent the kind of person you want to be – both in mind and body. You can include things like photos of your family and friends, or pictures that represent your dream career. I love to include inspiring quotes on my Vision Board too, like the ones I listed in chapter 10.

Just like when you write down dreams in words, when you see a visual representation of your dreams every day, you become familiar with them and what success would look like.

You just seem to open yourself up to opportunities and find ways to make them come true. You attract the right things and understand how to say no to the things that don't matter.

Now this is really important. Put your Vision Board somewhere where you will see it daily. Staying connected to your dreams is so important when you're deep in making them happen. Seeing your Dream Vision Board daily is key to that.

I also use what I call my Vision Board Book that I can take with me when I travel. It's a simple A4 spiral notebook and in it I have different pages for my different life areas – like we explored previously in the dreaming exercises. These include my dreams in writing, inspirational quotes, pictures, and anything else that motivates me and reminds me of what I'm working towards. For example:

+ I have pages for my fitness and health, including pages on nutrition and food, body, mind and spirituality.
+ I have pages for my business, which include dreams for the kikki.K future, a mind map of all the things I'd love to do, countries, collaborations and product ideas, mentors and business people I'd love to meet, and other business ideas.
+ For my personal development pages, I have books I want to read, courses I want to take, quotes, inspirational ideas, podcasts I want to listen to and people in this space I want to meet.
+ For my family pages, I have photos of us travelling, things we want to do as a family – our family dreams, notes on the kind of partner and mother I want to be, and a page on the kind of daughter, sister and daughter-in-law I want to be.

And that's just the start. I also have pages for my friends, travel, finances, home, my morning ritual and my ten-year plan. I love it!

Whether you create big vision boards or a vision board book (or both like me), choose whatever works best for you. A vision board is a great way to create inspiration at home and empower you to keep going. And the vision board book is something you can scribble notes in, add to each day and keep with you no matter where you are.

Another way of doing this is to create a screensaver or phone background so that your dreams are in front of you daily. Some people I know wear a special piece of jewellery or use other symbols to remind them daily of their dreams. Others I know laminate their dreams and stick them up on their shower wall.

Whichever way you do it, take time daily to really stop and look at what you've created to remind you of your dreams. Take time to immerse yourself in that visualisation of your future.

TO CREATE YOUR VISION BOARD, THIS IS WHAT YOU'LL NEED:

+ A VISION BOARD OR BOOK (BLANK A4 NOTEBOOK)[24]
+ PUSH PINS (FOR THE BOARD), GLUE OR DOUBLE-SIDED STICKY TAPE (FOR THE BOOK) AND SCISSORS[24]
+ MAGAZINES, PHOTOS, IMAGES
+ INSPIRING QUOTES OR QUOTE CARDS[24]

When you're creating, consider all the dreams you've explored earlier – your 101 Dreams List and your Dream Life Blueprint divided into life areas. Look back at the Dream Life Story you created for yourself in chapter 13. Capture inspiration for the top three dreams that you chose to focus on first, and then add inspirational visual reminders for others too, if and when you want to.

As you start to turn your dreams into reality, refine your Vision Board and/or Book. Check in on your progress. What have you achieved? What is on its way to coming true? Where do you still need to take action?

---

24   AVAILABLE FROM KIKKI.K STORES OR AT WWW.KIKKI-K.COM

THE FUTURE BELONGS TO THOSE

WHO BELIEVE IN THE BEAUTY

OF THEIR DREAMS.

- ELEANOR ROOSEVELT -

EXERCISE

01 /

SCHEDULE TIME IN YOUR DIARY OR CALENDAR
TO CREATE YOUR VISION BOARD AND/OR
VISION BOARD BOOK.

02 /

WRITE AT LEAST THREE OF YOUR FAVOURITE
DREAMS ON YOUR VISION BOARD (OR CREATE
PAGES FOR EACH IF USING A VISION BOARD
BOOK). THEN ADD PICTURES, WORDS AND
QUOTES THAT RESONATE WITH YOU AND WILL
INSPIRE YOU ON YOUR JOURNEY TOWARDS
YOUR DREAM LIFE.

03 /

PLACE YOUR VISION BOARD/BOOK WHERE
YOU'LL SEE IT DAILY. ADD TO IT AS YOU FIND
NEW SOURCES OF INSPIRATION.

04 /

IF YOU FEEL OKAY ABOUT IT GIVEN YOUR
PERSONAL CIRCUMSTANCES, SHARE YOUR
WORK WITH ME AND OUR COMMUNITY OF
DREAMERS BY TAKING A PHOTO AND SHARING
IT VIA @KRISTINAKIKKIK AND
@KIKKI.K – USING #KIKKIKDREAMLIFE AND
#101MILLIONDREAMERS. WE'D LOVE TO SEE
YOUR DREAMS SO WE CAN KEEP EACH OTHER
INSPIRED AND MOTIVATED ALONG THE WAY.

LOOK AT YOUR DREAMS DAILY

1 CREATING A VISUAL REPRESENTATION OF YOUR DREAMS IS SO IMPORTANT TO HELP YOU STAY MOTIVATED AND TAKE ACTION TO TURN THEM INTO REALITY

2 WHEN YOU SEE YOUR DREAMS DAILY, YOU START TO OPEN YOURSELF UP TO OPPORTUNITIES AND TAKE ACTIONS CONSCIOUSLY AND SUBCONSCIOUSLY TO MAKE THEM COME TRUE

16

THE ENORMOUS POWER OF SHARING YOUR DREAMS

YOUR DREAM LIFE STARTS HERE

As you have experienced, writing down your dreams is so very potent. It grounds the dream – making it very real – and helps you open yourself up to new opportunities that will take you towards that dream.

For similar reasons, when you go a step further and actually share your dreams with other people, there is even more power.

But the big difference is the vulnerability involved in sharing, the power of the feedback you get once you share and the inspiration you give to other people. My experience is that it makes dreams even more real and stronger for you – almost giving them a life of their own.

Actually saying your dreams aloud to other people will cause you to question them (and yourself!), to reflect on them, possibly edit them – and then commit even more deeply to them.

It also means that in some way you become accountable to someone else. You're putting your integrity on the line. While this can be scary, my experience is that while some people may not be overly supportive or excited for you, the right people will give you amazing support – and there is so much strength to be gained from that and from the sense of commitment that comes after sharing.

I remember vividly a day when a journalist was interviewing me about the growth of kikki.K. It was in our early days and from memory we had three stores. The interview was going really well when the journalist asked me, 'How many stores do you plan to have?' I froze inside.

We'd been working towards our big dream of having kikki.K stores in all my favourite cities around the world, but could I really tell a journalist that?! We had only just increased our initial written business plan for the next few years from twelve stores to forty stores nationwide. Could I really tell her that I planned to open forty stores? I could hardly even contemplate how big a dream that was – despite my real global dream being so very much bigger than that – let alone say it out loud to a journalist.

With all the confidence I could muster, I replied that our plan was to have forty stores in the next few years. Yep, forty stores. The journalist didn't skip a beat. That dream didn't seem too big to her. She just moved on to the next question and I regained my composure.

When the interview finished, and I was driving home, a sense of panic and self-doubt gripped me. Did I really say that? Did I really tell a journalist that I was going to have forty stores in a few years? Oh my! How vulnerable I felt. Was I a fraud? Could I really make that happen?

But by the time I got home that night, I'd had time to process it and was feeling much better. The terrifying experience of sharing my dream with someone, especially someone in the media, had made me look long and hard at that dream.

I thought through the reasons why I was chasing it. I thought of all the reasons why I truly believed it was possible. I thought through the risks and uncertainty. I thought through what really mattered to me. As a result, I felt so much stronger in my beliefs and my commitment to that dream. (It's particularly funny to think back on this story given we now have more than 100 stores of our own and we're stocked in hundreds more.)

When the article was published, it was very complimentary and the phone started ringing with landlords saying they had read the article, they loved kikki.K and they wanted their shopping centre to be one of the forty with a kikki.K store. They even offered favourable deals and incentives for us to open a store in their centres.

Of course, I'm not saying to go straight out and share your dream with a journalist, unless you feel that's appropriate. What I *am* saying is that there is power in sharing. There's power in being vulnerable – with the right people and for the right reasons.

Something to keep in mind: positive feedback about your dream makes you feel great, but you also need to be realistic when you do receive it. For instance, your friends and family will often want to say only nice things and avoid challenging your dreams, but challenge is fantastic and should be welcomed.

One incident from my early days in business still resonates with me. It was not long after our first store opened that I shared my big dream of opening kikki.K stores around the world with a close friend, who was very supportive. He, in turn, talked about it with a mutual acquaintance who said, 'No, that's not possible. She won't be able to do that.'

My close friend was concerned and told me what our acquaintance had said. I felt sick. I felt like my balloon had been popped. But before long, the self-doubts it raised for me had an amazing outcome.

I questioned my dream yet again. It stood up to this scrutiny and I came out feeling much stronger in my beliefs. In a strange way, it also gave me a greater will to make kikki.K succeed. There's so much motivating power in wanting 'to show them I can do it' and it became an issue of integrity for me to prove to others that my dream was valid. In a small way, those negative comments really fuelled me for a time.

The kikki.K 101 Dreams workshops that I've run with thousands of people in cities around the world – during which I help people write down dreams from their hearts and share them – have taught me so many other lessons too. As we explored in chapter 2, it can be a real source of inspiration to hear about other people's dreams.

It's amazing what happens in these workshops when I first ask people to share their dreams. Most times, the room falls quiet and people start looking at the floor or coughing nervously! Then a few brave souls put up their hands...

As they start to speak, the atmosphere lightens. Yes. We hear you! Soon, everyone is oohing and aahing in sincere support. They start jostling for the chance to share their dreams too, and at nearly every workshop, people tell me afterwards they were inspired by the dreams of others to reimagine their own dreams and to dream bigger. The other thing that always happens is that people step forward and offer assistance to make the dreams of others come true. Magic happens! It's one of the reasons I'm so inspired to chase my dream of inspiring 101 million people around the world to dream. The ripple effect of that will be so positive.

A great example of this happened recently at a dream workshop I hosted with a large group in London. After taking the group through the 101 Dreams exercise, I invited people to stand up and share one dream with the audience. After the normal long pause as people summoned the courage to step up, a lovely woman stood and told us that her dream was to write a children's book.

She had a great story of being inspired by her own children, shared her book idea with us all and confessed that she just wasn't sure where to start. Moments later, a person on the other side of the room stood up and said, 'I'm a children's book publisher. Let's have coffee tomorrow!'

I see this time and time again, and it's so rewarding to be part of inspiring thousands of people around the world to discover their dreams – and in many cases, to rediscover dreaming. In the Philippines recently, after hosting a 101 Dreams workshop, a lady approached me and was excited to tell me that as a young woman she had actively dreamed and set about making those dreams a reality. But, like many others, over time she had just forgotten to pull herself out of her day-to-day life, to pause and take time to reimagine her future and create new dreams. She was so grateful to have been inspired to get back to that and was buzzing with excitement.

Which brings me to my next point. Magic really does happen when you share a dream – when you put a dream out into the universe, you are often taking a vital step along the path towards making that dream a reality.

Serendipity is one of my favourite English words, and I've seen it happen so often when people begin to share their dreams. Thinking of opening a cafe? The friend you told about your dream just happens to know the perfect place. It always surprises me what appears when you tell others what you're seeking. Most people are incredibly supportive and willing to help in whatever way they can.

Imagine too what impact sharing your dream could have on others – how it might inspire them. Perhaps hearing you talk about your dream life will encourage them to contemplate theirs too.

I'll never forget when, shortly after my partner Paul shared some dreams with a young friend of ours, Mathilda, she came back with tears in her eyes to tell us she now knew for sure that she wanted to make a dream of hers happen – to try to have children. It was a thought she'd been toying with, but not paying much attention to – but then, inspired by hearing some of Paul's dreams, she now knew this was a key part of the life she wanted to create. Sharing your dreams with others will inspire them to dream too – sending out ripples of positivity and possibility to the world.

So how can you harness the power of dream sharing in your own life? I've found it really useful to think deeply about the following questions. Just remember, it's not all about what you do, but also what you choose *not* to do.

IN YOUR DREAM LIFE JOURNAL:

01 /

THINK ABOUT THE PEOPLE CLOSE TO YOU. WHO COULD YOU SHARE YOUR TOP THREE DREAMS WITH? WRITE DOWN THOSE IN YOUR NETWORK (FAMILY, FRIENDS, COLLEAGUES, MENTORS) YOU KNOW WILL LISTEN, BE INTERESTED AND OFFER SUPPORT - EVEN IF AT TIMES YOU KNOW THEY WILL CHALLENGE YOU. SHARE WITH THEM IF IT FEELS RIGHT.

02 /

WHO WOULD YOU DEFINITELY *NOT* SHARE YOUR DREAMS WITH? WHY?

03 /

THINK OF OTHER WAYS YOU COULD SHARE YOUR DREAMS AND SEEK FEEDBACK. CONSIDER SETTING UP YOUR OWN DREAM GROUP. IS THAT SOMETHING YOU'RE READY TO DO NOW THAT YOU'VE COME SO FAR ALONG YOUR OWN JOURNEY TOWARDS YOUR DREAM LIFE?

04 /

LATER IN THE BOOK WE'LL INVITE YOU TO CONSIDER SHARING YOUR DREAMS WITH OUR GLOBAL COMMUNITY OF DREAMERS - TO INSPIRE OTHERS AND TO POTENTIALLY RECEIVE FEEDBACK FROM OTHER LIKE-MINDED PEOPLE. THINK ABOUT WHETHER THAT'S SOMETHING THAT FEELS RIGHT FOR YOU GIVEN YOUR PERSONAL CIRCUMSTANCES AND ONLY DO IT IF IT FEELS RIGHT FOR YOU. BE SURE TO TAP INTO ONGOING INSPIRATION FROM THE DREAMS AND STORIES OF OTHERS BY SUBSCRIBING TO MY PODCASTS AND BLOG VIA WWW.KIKKI-K.COM/DREAMLIFE AND BY FOLLOWING THE HASHTAGS #KIKKIKDREAMLIFE AND #101MILLIONDREAMERS.

THE ENORMOUS POWER OF SHARING YOUR DREAMS

1 SHARING YOUR DREAMS WITH OTHERS WILL MAKE YOU ACCOUNTABLE AND HELP YOU ACHIEVE THEM

2 OPENING YOURSELF UP TO THE SUPPORT (AND NETWORKS) OF OTHERS OPENS DOORS YOU CANNOT IMAGINE

3 SURROUNDING YOURSELF WITH THE RIGHT PEOPLE WILL GIVE YOU ENERGY AND SUPPORT YOU ON YOUR JOURNEY TOWARDS YOUR DREAM LIFE

'VERY FEW PEOPLE EVER MADE A GREAT IDEA COME TO LIFE WITHOUT A LOT OF HELP.'

SIR RICHARD BRANSON

'm a big fan of Sir Richard Branson. If you don't know about him, he's the English business magnate, adventurer, investor and philanthropist who founded the Virgin Group and has started more than 400 companies.

His story is so inspiring for me because it shows how far your dreams can take you, one dream at a time. I can't imagine he ever thought at the age of sixteen when he launched his first business venture – a magazine called *Student* – that he would end up with an airline (Virgin Atlantic), a music label (Virgin Records), a chain of record stores (Virgin Megastores) and a spaceflight company (Virgin Galactic). No wonder the Queen knighted him for 'services to entrepreneurship'.

As I mentioned earlier in the book, I was lucky enough to make my dream to meet Richard come true. I found him to be very humble and even more inspiring in person than I'd expected – and my expectations were high. One thing that struck me in particular was that after all his success, it was amazing to see him on the edge of his seat listening to the speakers at the small conference we were at together. He was furiously hand-writing notes, still so very focused on learning.

I love his views on dreaming – the way he talks about the story of his success being 'a tale of big dreams' – and I'm grateful he agreed I could share them here with you.

In Richard's words, 'Dreaming is one of humanity's greatest gifts. It champions aspiration, spurs innovation, leads to change and propels us forward. In a world without dreams, there would be no adventure, no moon landing … no civil rights. What a half-lived and tragic existence we would have. We should all dream big, and encourage others to do so, too.'

Despite facing many obstacles in his life – from surviving several near fatal hot air balloon crashes (as he attempted and eventually succeeded with various record breaking flights) to seeing his company through difficult legal battles and big setbacks to his spaceflight plans – he's a person who is forever optimistic about chasing his dreams.

'The odds have often been stacked against us,' he wrote recently on his Virgin.com blog,[25] 'but by not limiting ourselves to what we have been told to be true, we have been able to make the impossible possible.'

I love the four key tips on dreaming he recently shared, very much in line with the approaches you are practising in this book.

Schedule time to dream

In the same way you make time in life for various events and meetings, open your calendar and schedule time just to dream. So important.

Don't be self-conscious

'Don't be self-conscious about dreaming, or about people thinking you're too idealistic, and not serious enough,' Branson says. 'Don't allow your self-talk to be judgemental.'

Be scared, but not scared off

'If your dreams don't scare you, they are too small. But those who achieve great things are the ones willing to be scared but not scared off.' Quoting George Addair, he adds: 'Everything you've ever wanted is on the other side of fear.'

Be open to receiving help from others

It's Richard's final point that is the reason I've included his story here after the chapter on sharing, because it is so, so important when you are setting out on your dreaming journey.

'If you share your dream with like-minded people who share your passion, you could take your dream places you never imagined going,' he says.

And he should know.

25 BRANSON, RICHARD. 'HOW TO DREAM BIG,' VIRGIN.COM (BLOG), VIRGIN, AUGUST 28, 2017, HTTPS://WWW.VIRGIN.COM/RICHARD-BRANSON/HOW-DREAM-BIG

Let Richard's story and tips inspire you to dream. Take some time now while it's fresh in your mind to ponder on it and, in the space below, or in your Dream Life Journal, write down anything you've learnt that you could apply in your own life.

PASSION IS ENERGY.

FEEL THE POWER THAT

COMES FROM FOCUSING

ON WHAT EXCITES YOU.

- OPRAH WINFREY -

17

FROM DREAMING TO DOING

YOUR DREAM LIFE STARTS HERE

Our journey started with you tapping into your heart, using the practi of unconstrained dreaming to start discovering your dream life. Since then you've been through an amazing process to refine and prioritise your dreams, and to write a simple and clear story describing how your dream life will look and feel. Now it's time to switch gears and move to making it happen.

Dreaming is wonderful, but it will only take you so far. You have to actually do the work to make your dreams a reality. I call it moving from 'Dreaming to Doing'. And this is what we'll be focusing on now – a simple process I use that will help you get started quickly on actually building your dream life.

But, before moving to doing, I want to share three of my most important learnings with you.

Firstly, you have to make sure you enjoy the process – that you enjoy everyday living and the beautiful little things in life while you're working towards your dreams.

Secondly, as you dream, do and enjoy, remember to share. Share your learnings, your time, your good fortune. Give to others along the way. Tie your dreams to the betterment of others. My experience is that what you give to others is usually returned many times over, often in unexpected ways, and the meaning it will give you makes life so much richer.

Finally, you need to cultivate the true belief that you can achieve your dreams. I love this quote from Walter Bonatti, a famous alpinist:

'WHEN YOU HAVE EXTRAORDINARY DREAMS, WHEN YOU REALLY BELIEVE YOU CAN MAKE THEM COME TRUE, ONLY THEN DOES YOUR MIND OVERCOME THE BARRIER OF THE IMPOSSIBLE.'

And now, back to doing...

There's so much to learn about how to make dreams happen – in fact, that's the subject of an entirely new book that I'm currently working on – but for now I want to just keep you moving forward to the next key step, moving from dreaming to doing.

We'll be taking your big, amazing dreams and dividing them up into smaller, actionable steps. Making the impossible possible. In the remaining chapters, we're going to build on everything you've done so far in our journey together. We're going to take those three prioritised dreams that you identified in the previous chapter and show you how to turn each of these into seven clear and specific key actions to get you focused and moving forward on the most critical things you need to do.

There are so many ways to go about getting dreams achieved. Some people don't need much formal structure because their dreams are just so powerful and they have such strong reasons for wanting to make them a reality that they simply push forward and manage to find a way. But I want to share the simplest, most effective approach I've found based on my experience and the experiences of the many people from whom I've learnt.

To move effectively from dreaming to doing, we're going to run through a simple process with your prioritised dreams over the next chapters. We're going to rewrite your three dreams as Inspiringly SMART Dreams – the starting point for making them achievable. We'll run through a really simple and effective process of taking just one of your dreams and writing down every actionable step you need to take to make that dream a reality.

Then, because you can do anything, but not everything all at once, I'll help you pick out the top seven most important actionable steps from this big list. This is what you'll focus on – the few critical things into which you need to put your energy.

However, before all of that, now is a perfect time for you to take a deep breath. Literally. You're moving out of the beautiful heart-driven space of dreaming, creating and visualising. It's quite a change in the rhythm of this process, so before we move into what I believe is the most exciting part – the doing and enjoying – I want you to just stop, take some time out and reflect on how far you've come.

It's such an important point in your journey. Let's stop to savour it and enjoy it.

A DREAM WITHOUT

A PLAN IS

JUST A WISH.

- KATHERINE PATERSON -

EXERCISE

IN YOUR INSPIRING SPACE:

01 /

GO BACK AND GLANCE OVER EVERYTHING YOU'VE WRITTEN DOWN IN YOUR DREAM LIFE JOURNAL
SO FAR, ALL OF YOUR OUTPUT FROM THE EXERCISES.

_____

02 /

AS YOU DO THAT, REFLECT ON THE PROGRESS YOU'VE MADE AND HOW THAT MAKES YOU FEEL.
TAKE TIME TO CELEBRATE YOURSELF. TAKE TIME TO ENJOY.

_____

03 /

IF YOU'VE TEAMED UP WITH SOMEONE ELSE, TAKE SOME TIME TOGETHER TO CHAT AND REFLECT
ON WHAT YOU'VE LEARNT AND HOW FAR YOU'VE COME.

_____

04 /

WRITE DOWN ON A SEPARATE SHEET OF PAPER (NOT IN YOUR DREAM LIFE JOURNAL) ANY DOUBTS
YOU HAVE ABOUT YOUR DREAMS, OR YOUR ABILITY TO ACHIEVE THEM. ANY SELF-DOUBTS.
BRAINSTORM AS MANY THINGS AS YOU CAN POSSIBLY CAN.

WHEN YOU'RE DONE, TEAR THE PAPER INTO AS MANY SMALL PIECES AS YOU CAN AND TAKE
PLEASURE IN THROWING THEM INTO YOUR BIN AS YOU FEEL A SYMBOLIC SENSE OF RELIEF FROM
CASTING AWAY THE LIMITATION OF SELF-DOUBT. THIS IS A GREAT EXERCISE TO DO EVERY THREE
MONTHS, OR MORE OFTEN. PUT A REMINDER IN YOUR DIARY IF YOU WANT TO DO THAT.

FROM DREAMING TO DOING

1 IF YOU WANT TO MAKE
YOUR DREAMS COME TRUE,
YOU ACTUALLY HAVE TO
DO THE WORK!

2 BE SURE TO ENJOY
THE PROCESS

3 TIE YOUR DREAMS TO THE
BETTERMENT OF OTHERS

'BIG DREAM, LITTLE STEPS...'

KRISTINA KARLSSON

At this point in your journey towards creating your dream life, I want to share a little more of my personal story to show how you can have a big dream, and start with little steps first. It's a good segue into the rest of this book, which focuses on the doing – on breaking your dreams down into the simple steps required to achieve them.

Winding back the clock... It all really started for me at twenty-two years of age, with my 3am List of simple dreams – the story I shared at the start of this book. That was really the first time in my life that I had written my dreams on paper and experienced the remarkable power of that one simple practice.

That then eventually led me to come up with my big dream of opening beautiful Swedish stationery and design stores in all of my favourite cities around the world – and to start kikki.K. From that point in my life, I can honestly say I have in every way been living my dream life (which, of course, doesn't mean a perfect life!)

But what did I actually do to move from creating that big dream to making it happen? What were the first steps?

It was so simple and so basic. Anyone could have done it.

The day after my light bulb moment to start kikki.K, I wasn't sure where to start, so I just started. I simply opened the Yellow Pages business directory and looked under 'S' for stationery. There was so much I didn't know, but it didn't matter. What mattered was just making a start.

I read through every business listing in the stationery section and marked the ones that looked interesting. I still remember ticking the ones I wanted to see.

I had a rough idea of the types of products I wanted to create in my first range – simple and colourful matching notebooks, journals, storage boxes and folders. The basic products you find in a home office or workspace, but thoughtfully designed and, when used together, would match the style and fashion sense of the person using that space. I wanted to create a range that would make people's workspaces look and feel coordinated, inspiringly organised and beautiful. I wanted to make a positive impact on people's productivity and wellbeing.

I circled a lot of potential suppliers in the Yellow Pages, rang them, told them my dream and asked if I could come and visit them. I vividly remember my first few calls. I felt so excited, but initially also unusually nervous and shy about sharing my dream. But the more I said it out loud on the phone, the more comfortable I became with it, and the more real and compelling it became for me.

Unsurprisingly some of the people I spoke with just couldn't relate at all to my big dream, and must have thought I was a little strange. I got a few 'no's'. But nearly every one of those suppliers I rang booked me in for meetings. I was off and running, and right then it felt like I was living my dream life! I felt so alive. So happy. So excited. I was totally buzzing. What a change that was to how I was feeling before my 3am moment, when frustration and discontent were my overwhelming feelings.

I so hope this book helps you experience a transformation like this too.

I remember so clearly the many factories and offices I visited, and the looks on people's faces when I told them my dream again, about wanting to open beautiful stationery stores around the world – yet I had not even the most basic idea of how a notebook was made. Some laughed. Some were dismissive. Others just looked bemused. But some seemed to find my passion compelling. I later became the biggest customer of someone who had initially laughed at me – and I joked with him for years about that.

I don't think many took me seriously, but maybe out of curiosity or politeness, they showed me samples, toured me around their factories and explained the various processes of manufacture as I oohed and aahed and giggled with excitement! As a stationery lover with a big dream, I was simply in heaven. It was all so exciting – every little moment. I literally jumped up and down with joy in many of those early encounters, confirming to a lot of those people that I was more than a little crazy. And I was – but in a good way!

While doing all of this exploring, learning – and eventually developing my range – I supported myself financially by working two jobs. The first involved breakfast shifts as a waitress in a local hotel – leaving home at 4:30am to start at 5am, so I could finish by 9am and get on with my kikki.K work during the day. The second job was as a promotions girl, working nights and weekends hosting events. I never thought I would admit this, but one of those events involved me having to dress up as a rooster in a hideous outfit. Another had me in a way-too-tight silver-white jumpsuit. Both were slightly humiliating, but my focus was on doing what I had to do to earn money so I could live and make my dream happen.

I enrolled at a local college to do a course in writing a business plan, but eventually decided that just wasn't for me. As much as I tried, I just couldn't get my head around what they were teaching me to do. I got bogged down in all of the detail and lost patience with it.

I knew the planning was important, but it definitely wasn't a strength of mine and so I forced myself to think 'Who?' Who do I know who could help me with this?

The answer was reasonably simple – my partner Paul. So I enlisted his help, and eventually searched out various other people – friends and friends of friends – who had experience working in or building fashion labels and retail businesses. With their combined help, I developed a business plan and that started my habit of always searching out and learning from people who had done whatever it was that I wanted to do...

I learnt so much from these simple early steps – each one taking me forward. None of those small steps on their own were too hard to accomplish. I had started. I was learning. I was moving towards my dream.

Over dinner at the home of lovely friends of ours – Phil and Michele – I shared my dream and plans for kikki.K. Phil, a graphic designer, insisted on creating a logo for me then and there. His enthusiasm as he got caught up in my dream was so exciting for me, and with a bottle of wine by our side, we huddled around as I sketched on a paper serviette, sharing ideas as the logo took shape. He then created a few versions on his Mac including the logo we still use today. And that's yet another example of the often unexpected benefits that manifest when you share your dreams with the right people.

Eventually I designed a range and had a collection of samples made.

I can hardly explain my excitement when I picked up the first sample products. I couldn't wait for them to be delivered. I had to see them being finished off and packed for me. I wanted to touch them, smell them, lay them out on shelves together... I could have spent entire days simply looking and playing with these beautiful products! It felt like my dream had come true on the spot. I was in my own stationery heaven!

Now it was finally time to take my beautiful kikki.K brand and range 'to the world'. Well, to a few friends and friends of friends in my little corner of the world anyway!

I invited a group of friends to my home for the very first showing of kikki.K. The world premiere! I set up my sample range in my lounge room, in colour blocked style, taking hours to get it just right. Fussing over every detail. Wine and champagne were served on arrival and then I launched into my spiel – explaining the products, showing how they would work together to help stylish people create beautifully organised workspaces, and sharing my dream to open kikki.K stores around the world.

They loved it all – and so did I. I received so much positive feedback that I was convinced I was already made. Opening kikki.K stores around the world was going to be doable. I remember feeling on top of the world that night. The magic of dreams coming true. I was absolutely living my dream life. It was the change I wanted and had consciously decided to take. An eternity away from my frustration with life before my 3am List.

But when I woke in the morning, I had a clear realisation. My first stumbling block. My nearest and dearest friends had convinced me that my dream would work – but they were my friends, and they'd been drinking champagne. Would they really buy the products? Would other people buy the products? Would anyone want to buy high-quality, fashionable and premium-priced stationery?

In the cold, hard light of a new day, it all sounded too good to be true. What should I do? It was too premature to open a shop and I didn't have the money to do that anyway...

I thought it over and decided I had to find a way to keep testing. My solution was to run similar range showings as the first one I'd done, but this time with a difference. I would invite people I didn't know and I would offer the products for sale and see if people would actually buy anything.

I had very little money of my own so, as mentioned previously, I borrowed $3,000 from Paul and invested in a small order of about ten products in four colours each. I remember it felt a little scary, but totally exhilarating to invest in inventory (a new word for me back then!) It was another small step, and an incredibly exciting one.

A few of my first suppliers wanted to charge what I thought was too much to put on my logo – a very labour-intensive process for them in those days – so I decided I could do this myself. I enlisted the help of Paul and other good friends. One by one, we applied kikki.K logo stickers to hundreds of products and as we did, we chatted about how exciting it all was.

My dear friend, Penny Dann, was the first to offer to invite ten of her friends to her home to the first-ever kikki.K at Home event. I followed a similar format to the first showing I had done. I remember arriving early to set up my range in Penny's lounge room. Carrying the boxes of product out of my car. Feeling very excited, but a little anxious.

I so wanted it to go well. I wanted to set it all up beautifully. I wanted people to fall in love with kikki.K and I so hoped that they would buy even just a few products to give me proof that my dream was valid.

We had champagne on arrival. Some nervous chatter before starting.

Then I stood in front of a group of new friends and I shared my dream. I demonstrated my range and I finished by offering the products for sale. Then I held my breath...

They loved it! People queued up wanting to buy. I didn't know whom to serve first. I was in business – and it was thrilling. I sold more than I could have dreamed of and it was delightful to see people as excited as I was about kikki.K.

That night, as I drove home, the enormity of my dream dawned on me momentarily. I had no real idea how I was going to make it happen and I couldn't have cared less! I was up and running. I was loving what I was doing – I couldn't call it work – it was all fun. Even the hard stuff. I was living my dream life.

I went on to do another forty of those events. In people's homes in the evening. In offices at lunchtime. And I sold my range at various design markets. All of those were small steps. Each step gave me confidence, provided learnings and took me forward.

There are so many other stories I could share with you. My first office. First hire. The first time I ran out of cash. First bank loan. First investor. First store opening, and how we sold Paul's house to pay for it. The day I hit on my dream to inspire and empower 101 million people around the world to dream. The 100th store opening. The time I left new investors hanging, as I was meant to be signing a contract, but instead rushed away excited to see the new samples that had arrived at the office door...

But I just want you to know it all started with a dream – from my heart – and progressed by me just starting. Taking simple small steps. Following my passion. Doing what I love. Enjoying the journey. Following a purpose to inspire and empower the world. And just working it out along the way.

I wish I had this book as a guide back when I started, but I do now. And guess what? Even now, this book is proving so valuable to me.

I've been using it and the exercises I've compiled and improved as my guide, and getting amazing results.

Take some time now while it's fresh in your mind to ponder on my story – particularly the concept of breaking down your dream into small steps – and, in the space on the opposite page, or in your Dream Life Journal, write down anything you've learnt that you could apply in your own life.

THE ONLY WAY TO ACHIEVE THE
IMPOSSIBLE IS TO BELIEVE IT IS POSSIBLE.

- FROM *ALICE THROUGH THE LOOKING GLASS* -

CHAPTER EIGHTEEN

REWRITE YOUR DREAMS AS INSPIRINGLY
SMART DREAMS

YOUR DREAM LIFE STARTS HERE

I'm so excited for you as you move to doing, and now that you've had a chance to reflect, let's dive right in.

Dreams by nature are big and lofty and often unspecific, which is totally okay. In contrast, goals are clearer, measurable and time-specific, which is exactly what you need to help you move from dreaming to doing.

You may have heard people refer to SMART goals. My process involves using learnings from SMART goal setting and applying them to dreaming – in other words, you're going to be rewriting your high-level dreams into what I call Inspiringly SMART Dreams.

It's simple and it's important.

We talked earlier about the benefits of writing down your dreams, and the same benefits apply to rewriting your dreams as Inspiringly SMART Dreams.

The process of rewriting gets you to slow down a little – to think more deeply and acknowledge the importance of what you want to achieve. And by putting them on paper – this time in a more actionable way – you subconsciously (and consciously) start to take actions to achieve them. In this step in our process, your dreams really *do* have to be rewritten on paper.

More than that, you need to make sure your dreams are rewritten in a clear, inspiring and time-bound way – what I call an Inspiringly SMART way – which I'll explain more about below. This will force you to know exactly what you're setting out to achieve and by when. Yes, that means you need to take a big leap and *write down the date you will achieve your dream!*

Don't let this scare you. If the date drifts for a valid reason along the way, that's okay – you can change it. But at least start out with a completion date (which you just estimate to the best of your ability and knowledge today).

This is really important because, up to this point, your dreams have probably been written in general terms. Now, to bring them to life, you first need to make them clear, inspiring and give them a deadline.

Let me explain.

Word each dream as if you have already achieved it, and in a way that's positive, uplifting and inspiring. Why? You need to be able to *feel* what it will be like once you've achieved it. Wording dreams this way will excite you, pull you forward and make you feel great when you read them, when you think about them and when you talk about them.

As an example, let's take this popular dream: 'I want to eat more healthily.' (By the way, 37 per cent of Americans set this as a New Year's resolution for 2018).[26]

How much more positive, inspiring and uplifting is it to say: 'It's the 30th of June 2019 and I feel fantastic, full of energy and glowing with health because I'm now in the sustainable habit of following my healthy eating plan five days a week!'

Using positive language to rewrite your dream helps you really feel the benefits of what you're setting out to achieve. It's inspiring and can help you feel so strong as you do the hard work necessary to make it happen. Wording it as if it is already achieved helps bring the end into clear sight.

Make your dreams SMART. The concept of SMART goals has been around for some time and the way I apply it to dreams may be slightly different, but there's a reason it's still used by people all over the world. It works.

---

26 YOUGOV, DEC 8-11, 2017

SMART STANDS FOR:

- SPECIFIC
- MEASURABLE
- ATTAINABLE
- RELEVANT
- TIME-BOUND

What this means for you is that you need your dreams rewritten to be **Specific** (so you know what you're actually working towards). Big vague ideas are great for dreaming, but you need to get really specific when it comes to doing.

For example, if I think back on my personal journey, my initial dream was to 'open kikki.K stores in all my favourite cities around the world'. That was a big and inspiring dream – and has worked beautifully for me in many ways – but it wasn't super specific because initially it didn't need to be. Dreams are like that.

However, to help me work towards making that dream a reality, I had to break it down into smaller, doable SMART dreams. For example, I rewrote my dream at different times over the years, in much more specific ways like this: 'It's the 27th of August 2016, and I'm so excited and immensely proud that we just opened our very first store in an amazing location in London, and our guests love it!'

You also need to be able to know when you've actually achieved your dreams. When you rewrite them they need to be **Measurable**, so you know exactly *what* you're aiming to achieve and *when* you've achieved it.

In the example on the previous page, the measurable bits of the rewritten Inspiringly SMART Dream are the date, the reference to the store actually opening, it being in an amazing location and in what city, and also the reference to our guests loving it. Each of those things is measurable in some way.

The **Attainable** part of an Inspiringly SMART Dream is important because it's vital that you truly believe you can achieve it. That said, I know from firsthand experience that we can all achieve much more than we think we can, so it's really important to push yourself, aim high and get out of your comfort zone as you drive to achieve what your heart has helped you imagine for yourself.

Relevant means that your dreams need to be totally authentic to YOU and to YOUR dream life. Double check that your rewritten dreams really mean something to you, and that you own them 100 per cent. It's difficult to be 100 per cent committed to a dream that you set for someone else or solely because of someone else.

This is really important to remember, and I think one of the reasons the SMART approach is so successful.

Your dreams have to come from you and your heart. If something doesn't feel quite right when you're rewriting your dreams, then it probably *isn't* right. Spend time reflecting and making sure your dreams feel right and are important to you. My dreams won't be right for you, just as yours won't be right for me. Set ones you really care about and believe in – dreams that make YOU come alive. It's so important.

And lastly, your Inspiringly SMART Dreams have to be **Time-bound**. You have to give yourself a deadline and dates to work towards. If you set yourself dates to achieve each step, then you'll know exactly what you have to do and by when, and can organise your time around those commitments.

An aside worth thinking about here again is that one of the keys to achieving any dream is knowing *what not to do.* This frees you to focus on getting the most important things done.

When you do this, you really set yourself up for success and making your dreams SMART will help you with that.

Thinking back to my 3am List, it not only clearly outlined what I wanted, but also clearly implied what I didn't want. That list told me not to settle for a job I didn't enjoy, not to lose touch with my family and friends in Sweden, and not to assume that working for someone else was right for me.

Now let's walk through one more example of turning a high-level dream into an Inspiringly SMART Dream.

One of my recent top dreams came to me this year when I did the unconstrained dreaming exercise you did in chapter 1. My dream is 'to become the fittest I've ever been'.

You can see the way I first wrote down this dream wasn't overly specific and it didn't have a deadline. It wasn't written in the present tense as if I'd achieved it and it wasn't written in a way that was overly inspiring, uplifting or attractive for me. It certainly wasn't SMART. As we've covered earlier, that's okay for high-level dreams.

But to achieve dreams, we know they need to be rewritten as Inspiringly SMART Dreams so, using the guidelines above, this dream of mine became:

'It's the 7th of February 2019, I'm the fittest I've ever been by my three key measures. I feel strong, healthy, proud and energised because of it and have developed all of the habits and support systems I need to stay that way.'

Now it's your turn...

THE MAN WHO MOVES

A MOUNTAIN BEGINS

BY CARRYING AWAY

SMALL STONES.

- CONFUCIUS -

EXERCISE

01 /

REWRITE YOUR TOP THREE DREAMS AS INSPIRINGLY SMART DREAMS. REFER BACK TO THE EXPLANATION FOR GUIDANCE WHENEVER YOU NEED – AND TAKE YOUR TIME TO GET IT RIGHT FOR YOU.

SMART DREAM NO.1

_____

_____

_____

SMART DREAM NO.2

_____

_____

_____

SMART DREAM NO.3

_____

_____

_____

02 /

IF IT FEELS RIGHT FOR YOU GIVEN YOUR PERSONAL CIRCUMSTANCES, SHARE YOUR THREE DREAMS WITH ME AND OUR COMMUNITY OF DREAMERS BY TAKING A PHOTO OF THEM AND SHARING IT VIA @KRISTINAKIKKIK AND @KIKKI.K – USING #KIKKIKDREAMLIFE AND #101MILLIONDREAMERS. HOPEFULLY EITHER I, OR SOMEONE IN OUR COMMUNITY, WILL GET THE CHANCE TO COMMENT WITH ANY THOUGHTS THAT COULD HELP YOU ACHIEVE THEM. AND WE'D LOVE TO HEAR FROM YOU WHEN YOU ACHIEVE YOUR DREAMS, SO KEEP SHARING YOUR SUCCESSES AND ANY KEY LEARNINGS WITH US ALL TOO. WE CAN ALL LEARN FROM AND INSPIRE EACH OTHER.

REWRITE YOUR DREAMS
AS INSPIRINGLY SMART DREAMS

1 REWRITING YOUR DREAMS GETS YOU TO ACKNOWLEDGE THE IMPORTANCE OF WHAT YOU WANT TO ACHIEVE

2 WRITING DREAMS AS IF YOU HAVE ALREADY ACHIEVED THEM, AND IN A WAY THAT'S POSITIVE, UPLIFTING AND INSPIRING, HELPS YOU FEEL WHAT IT WILL BE LIKE TO ACHIEVE THEM

3 BY MAKING YOUR DREAMS SMART, YOU GIVE YOURSELF A FRAMEWORK FOR ACHIEVING THEM

4 KNOWING WHAT THINGS *NOT* TO DO HELPS YOU FOCUS ON GETTING THE MOST IMPORTANT THINGS DONE

19

BRAINSTORM EVERY ACTION

I just love the power and simplicity of brainstorming everything I can possibly do to make a dream a reality onto what I call my Master Action List. I simply write the now Inspiringly SMART Dream at the top of the page and then enjoy the freedom of just dumping down on paper every single thing I can think of...

Big things. Small things. Things I need to have to make it happen. Things I need to learn. Things I need to do. People I need to involve. Meetings I'll need to set up – both regular and one-off. Resources I need.

The lists are often long, but they flush out the many small steps that need to be taken to achieve the big dream. It's not rocket science. It's not complicated. It works.

I just write them all down in the order I think of them. I know some people find mind maps great for this and, if you do, then use that approach. My preference is a simple written list. I just let ideas pour out of me until I can't think of anything more.

This process moves me from worrying about where to start to actually just beginning. I don't get caught up in thinking about 'the doing', but just get every action step I can possibly think of onto paper – and it's so easy to do that.

I do this knowing that I'll sort through this Master Action List later, prioritise them all, select the most important, run them by any relevant people I need to involve, and then diarise them as bite-sized, doable actions.

You'll see an example on the following page.

MY DREAM:
TO BE THE FITTEST I HAVE EVER BEEN

AS AN INSPIRINGLY SMART DREAM:
IT'S THE 7TH OF FEBRUARY 2019, I'M THE FITTEST I'VE EVER BEEN BY MY THREE KEY MEASURES. I FEEL STRONG, HEALTHY, PROUD AND ENERGISED BECAUSE OF IT AND HAVE DEVELOPED ALL THE HABITS AND SUPPORT SYSTEMS I NEED TO STAY THAT WAY.

MY MASTER ACTION LIST:

+ SIGN UP FOR AN APP THAT I CAN USE IF I DON'T GET TO CLASSES
+ RESEARCH YOGA, PILATES AND GYMS IN MY AREA
+ DO A SCHEDULE AND BOOK CLASSES
+ FIND PODCASTS/BOOKS/BLOGS I CAN READ AND LISTEN TO, TO KEEP ME MOTIVATED
+ DECIDE IF I WANT A PERSONAL TRAINER/FITNESS COACH
+ SCHEDULE TIBETAN RITES INTO MY DIARY
+ CALL MY FRIEND'S YOGA TEACHER
+ SLEEP WELL SO I CAN GET UP EARLY
+ GET TO BED ON TIME REGULARLY AND SET ALARM TO GET UP ON TIME
+ SEE A NATUROPATH SO I EAT WELL TO SUPPORT MY FITNESS AND SEE IF I'M LOW ON ANYTHING
+ START MEASURING WHERE I'M AT AND MY PROGRESS THROUGH THE YEAR
+ DECIDE ON THE EXACT THREE MEASURES
+ PUT OUT EXERCISE CLOTHES BEFORE GOING TO BED
+ USE THE HABITS PAD TO TICK OFF MY EXERCISE DAILY
+ SPEAK TO REBECCA AND LEARN FROM HER – SHE IS MY FIT FRIEND!
+ WALK IN NATURE ONCE A WEEK
+ DO A 28-DAY DETOX TO INCREASE MY ENERGY
+ SET A DATE FOR A SPRING JUICE CLEANSE
+ MAINTAIN ALCOHOL-FREE NIGHTS SO I CAN GET UP ON TIME
+ START USING 5 KM APP WITH AXEL
+ LOOK AT MY FITNESS DREAM DAILY
+ CREATE A VISION BOARD FOR MY FITNESS DREAM
+ WHO CAN HELP SUPPORT ME? PT? FITNESS COACH? PAUL? REBECCA? HOW?
+ BOOK IN HALF AN HOUR IN DIARY TO FINISH MY LIST OF POTENTIAL BARRIERS AND HOW TO OVERCOME THEM
+ PUT UP MY DREAM ON THE BATHROOM MIRROR AND A CHART TO TICK OFF DAILY WHEN DONE
+ SHARE MY PLANS WITH THE FAMILY TO HELP KEEP ME ACCOUNTABLE/GIVE SUPPORT

So let's get to it!

IT IS BETTER TO HAVE ENOUGH

IDEAS FOR SOME OF THEM TO BE

WRONG, THAN TO BE ALWAYS RIGHT

BY HAVING NO IDEAS AT ALL.

- EDWARD DE BONO -

EXERCISE

IN YOUR DREAM LIFE JOURNAL (OR ON THE OPPOSITE PAGE):

01 /

CHOOSE ONE OF YOUR TOP THREE INSPIRINGLY SMART DREAMS AND WRITE IT AT THE TOP OF THE PAGE (YOUR MASTER ACTION LIST).

_____

02 /

UNDERNEATH THAT, LIST EVERYTHING YOU CAN POSSIBLY THINK OF THAT YOU NEED TO DO TO ACHIEVE YOUR DREAM. REFER TO MY EXAMPLE AS A GUIDE.

_____

03 /

DO THE SAME FOR YOUR OTHER DREAMS, WHENEVER YOU'RE READY FOR THAT.

WHEN YOU'VE RUN OUT OF IDEAS, IT'S TIME TO ASK YOURSELF THE KEY QUESTIONS IN THE FOLLOWING CHAPTERS. MORE OFTEN THAN NOT, THESE WILL DRAW OUT IMPORTANT ADDITIONAL THINGS THAT YOU WOULDN'T HAVE CONSIDERED OTHERWISE. YOU'LL NEED TO ADD THESE TO YOUR MASTER ACTION LISTS TO ENSURE YOU'RE AS EFFECTIVE AS POSSIBLE IN YOUR DOING.

EXERCISE

DREAM 1	DREAM 2	DREAM 3

1 BRAINSTORMING YOUR IDEAS – AND GETTING THEM DOWN ON PAPER – HELPS YOU START QUICKLY AND FLUSH OUT THE MANY SMALL STEPS YOU NEED TO TAKE TO ACHIEVE YOUR DREAM. IT ALSO HELPS AVOID PROCRASTINATION!

2 LETTING YOUR IDEAS FLOW WITHOUT CONSTRAINT IS A POWERFUL WAY OF CONNECTING WITH YOUR INTUITION AND IMAGINATION

20

WHO CAN HELP?

In my experience, one of the most important things you can possibly ask yourself when you're moving into the mode of getting things done is 'Who?'

Who can help me with this? Who has successfully done this before? Who can I learn from? Who can support me? Who could mentor me on this? Who can I include in my team to help me achieve this?

And maybe the most important 'Who?' question of all... Who can help me make this dream come true and may want to because they have a strong interest in the outcome?

There is so little that hasn't been done and there are so many people who can help you by sharing their experience. Reach out to them or study what they have done in whatever way you can.

And of course, if people do help you, always approach it as a win-win. Make sure you give back to them in whatever way you can and, when you get the chance to help others, take it. Helping others helps the world go around.

But a word of warning here. I want to share a very important thing that I've discovered over the years: Be very careful taking advice from people who have not done what you want to do. Those people will be giving you an opinion – which may or may not be right or useful – and it will not be based on hard-earned personal experience. Be careful to differentiate between valuable experience sharing and random advice!

Now let's take action...

EXERCISE

IN YOUR DREAM LIFE JOURNAL:

01 /

FOR EACH OF YOUR THREE PRIORITY DREAMS, TURN TO THE WORKSHEET TITLED 'WHO?' DOWN THE LEFT-HAND SIDE, LIST AS MANY PEOPLE YOU CAN THINK OF WHO MAY BE ABLE TO HELP YOU ACHIEVE YOUR DREAM IN SOME WAY. REFER BACK TO MY EXPLANATION AND QUESTIONS ON THE PREVIOUS PAGE AS YOU WRITE. (WE DID A SIMILAR EXERCISE EARLIER WHEN WE WERE LOOKING AT WHO YOU WANT TO MEET, IN GENERAL, TO GET INSPIRATION FROM. NOW WE'RE GETTING MORE SPECIFIC AND IT'S TIME TO WORK OUT WHO CAN HELP YOU ACHIEVE YOUR TOP THREE DREAMS.)

IF YOU'RE A LITTLE STUCK WITH WHERE TO START, ASK YOURSELF: 'WHO HAS ACHIEVED SOMETHING SIMILAR AND HOW CAN I LEARN FROM THEIR EXPERIENCE?' AND 'WHO CAN HELP ME MAKE THIS DREAM COME TRUE AND MAY WANT TO BECAUSE THEY HAVE A STRONG INTEREST IN THE OUTCOME?'

02 /

THEN IN THE NEXT COLUMN, WRITE DOWN WHY YOU WANT TO MEET EACH PERSON AND HOW YOU THINK THEY CAN HELP YOU.

03 /

IN THE LAST COLUMN, WRITE DOWN HOW YOU THINK YOU CAN GET IN CONTACT WITH EACH OF THOSE PEOPLE.

THIS IS A LIST THAT CAN STAY LIVE FOR YOU. ADD TO IT WHENEVER YOU NEED TO. AND DON'T FORGET TO ADD ANY ADDITIONAL ACTIONS YOU'VE COME UP WITH TO YOUR MASTER ACTION LISTS.

HERE'S AN EXAMPLE FROM MY LIST OF 'WHO CAN HELP WITH MY DREAM OF WRITING THIS BOOK', WHICH EVOLVED DURING THE WRITING PROCESS.

EXERCISE

DREAM: IT'S SEPTEMBER 2018 AND I WALK PAST A BOOKSHOP AND SEE MY BOOK DISPLAYED BEAUTIFULLY IN A BIG STACK ON THE BESTSELLERS TABLE. I FEEL PROUD AND SO EXCITED ABOUT THE MANY PEOPLE WHO WILL BE INSPIRED TO DISCOVER AND CREATE THEIR DREAM LIVES!

WHO?	WHY? WHAT CAN THEY HELP WITH?	HOW CAN I MEET THEM/LEARN FROM THEM?
AN EDITOR	OUR FIRST BOOK LIKE THIS – WILL DEFINITELY NEED HELP WITH EDITING! MY WRITTEN ENGLISH IS NOT GREAT!	ASK EVERYONE WE KNOW WHO HAS WRITTEN BOOKS FOR A LIST OF APPROPRIATE GREAT EDITORS – THEN CALL/MEET/SELECT.
DR LIBBY	HAS WRITTEN MANY BOOKS. KNOWS ABOUT THAT AND ABOUT PUBLISHING. HAS CREATED ONLINE LEARNING MODULES AS WELL AND HAS EXPERIENCE IN THAT FIELD.	CALL/EMAIL/MEET.
TERERAI	HAS DIRECT AND INCREDIBLE EXPERIENCE GOING FROM DREAMING TO DOING. OUR STORIES ARE SO DIFFERENT BUT HAVE SO MANY SIMILAR CONCEPTS TO TEACH/SHARE.	LISTEN TO/WATCH INTERVIEWS ONLINE. EMAIL HER. FIND A WAY TO MEET!
PUBLISHERS OF SIMILAR BOOKS	EXPLORE WHAT PUBLISHERS OFFER VERSUS ME SELF-PUBLISHING.	LOOK IN BOOKS I LOVE TO PUT TOGETHER A LIST OF APPROPRIATE PUBLISHERS. CALL THEM.
A RANGE OF PEOPLE WITH INSPIRING DREAM STORIES TO SHARE THAT FIT THE SCOPE OF MY BOOK	WOULD BE GREAT TO PRESENT A DIVERSE RANGE OF STORIES TO HELP READERS CONNECT WITH THE EXPERIENCE I WANT TO SHARE – AND HELP THEM GET A LOT OF VALUE FROM THE BOOK.	MAKE A LIST – SEE IF FRIENDS OR FRIENDS OF FRIENDS KNOW THEM.

KEEP AWAY FROM THOSE

WHO TRY TO BELITTLE YOUR

AMBITIONS. SMALL PEOPLE

ALWAYS DO THAT, BUT THE

REALLY GREAT MAKE YOU

FEEL THAT YOU TOO CAN

BECOME GREAT.

- MARK TWAIN -

WHO CAN HELP?

1 REACHING OUT TO PEOPLE WITH DIRECT PERSONAL EXPERIENCE IN YOUR AREA OF INTEREST WILL OPEN YOUR MIND TO IDEAS YOU MAY NEVER THINK OF OTHERWISE

2 LEARNING FROM OTHERS WILL GIVE YOU ENERGY AND SUPPORT YOU IN YOUR JOURNEY TOWARDS YOUR DREAM LIFE

3 GIVING BACK TO OTHERS – IN WHATEVER WAY YOU CAN – IS A GREAT WAY TO REPAY ALL THE HELP YOU RECEIVE ALONG THE WAY

4 ALWAYS THINK WIN-WIN

21

POTENTIAL BARRIERS AND
POSSIBLE SOLUTIONS

-GET CLEAR ON WHAT I DON'T KNOW THAT I NEED
TO KNOW
-TALK TO OTHERS WHO HAVE DONE THIS TO LEARN
HOW THEY MADE IT HAPPEN
-FIND LIKE-MINDED PEOPLE WHO CAN JOIN MY
SUPPORT TEAM OR MENTOR ME

I find it really useful as I'm planning to achieve my dreams to make a well-thought-out list of all of the potential barriers I might face – all the things I can think of that could stop me achieving my dream.

Then I take my time and think through ways I could avoid each of those barriers – well in advance. Thinking from this angle always helps me flush out different things I need to do and always prompts me with more great ideas for my Master Action List.

For example, a potential barrier for me when I'm working on a dream is that I can sometimes drift off track if I don't make myself accountable to other people (particularly with exercise!)

The one way I know I can avoid this is to make a commitment to other people. For my fitness dream, I recently gathered some friends together on a group message and we all committed to letting each other know when we've completed our planned exercise for the day.

My sense of integrity won't allow me to let them down, which helps me overcome the potential barrier of having to motivate myself. In effect, making myself accountable to others is a support for me to achieve what I want to achieve. We'll touch more on supports in the next chapter.

As an example to contemplate, on the following page are some common barriers I know people face that could be applicable to many different dreams. I've also included some possible solutions.

POTENTIAL BARRIERS	POSSIBLE SOLUTIONS
NEED LOTS OF TIME	ESTIMATE AS BEST I CAN HOW MUCH TIME I NEED AND HOW OFTEN. LOOK AT EVERYTHING I DO NOW THAT I COULD SPEND LESS TIME ON, TO MAKE MORE TIME. WHAT CAN I SAY NO TO?
DON'T HAVE ALL THE KNOWLEDGE OR EXPERIENCE I NEED	GET CLEAR ON WHAT I DON'T KNOW THAT I NEED TO KNOW. HOW CAN I LEARN WHAT I NEED? WHO CAN I LEARN FROM WHO HAS DONE THIS BEFORE? HOW? WHAT BOOKS? WHAT COURSES?
NEED LOTS OF CASH TO MAKE IT HAPPEN	DEFINE EXACTLY HOW MUCH. DEVELOP A CLEAR PLAN SHOWING THE INVESTMENT, RISKS, COSTS AND POSSIBLE BENEFITS. TALK TO OTHERS WHO HAVE DONE THIS TO LEARN HOW THEY MADE IT HAPPEN. PLAN TO EARN OR RAISE THE MONEY. FIND A LOW-COST WAY TO AT LEAST TEST THE IDEA.
FEAR OR LACK OF CONFIDENCE TO GO FOR IT	TALK WITH SOMEONE WHO HAS DONE WHAT I WANT TO DO. LEARN AS MUCH AS I CAN TO HELP ME UNDERSTAND WHAT'S REQUIRED TO HELP BUILD MY BELIEF THAT IT'S POSSIBLE FOR ME. READ *FEEL THE FEAR AND DO IT ANYWAY* BY SUSAN JEFFERS.[27]
UNSUPPORTIVE PEOPLE AROUND ME	FIND LIKE-MINDED PEOPLE WHO CAN JOIN MY SUPPORT TEAM OR MENTOR ME. SEEK OUT PEOPLE WHO HAVE EXPERIENCED SOMETHING SIMILAR AND ASK THEIR ADVICE (OR READ THEIR STORIES TO SEE WHAT I CAN LEARN). GET COMFORTABLE WITH TRUSTING MYSELF, NOT TAKING ON THE LIMITING INFLUENCES.
DON'T KNOW THE PEOPLE WITH THE KNOWLEDGE I NEED TO ACHIEVE MY DREAM	WRITE A LIST OF THE PEOPLE, OR TYPES OF PEOPLE, I NEED TO KNOW. ASK PEOPLE I KNOW IF THEY KNOW THEM – OR IF THEY KNOW ANYONE ELSE WHO KNOWS THEM AND CAN INTRODUCE ME.

27 SUSAN JEFFERS, *FEEL THE FEAR AND DO IT ANYWAY* (NEW YORK: BALLANTINE BOOKS, 1987)

EXERCISE

IN YOUR DREAM LIFE JOURNAL:

01 /

FIND THE 'POTENTIAL BARRIERS AND POSSIBLE SOLUTIONS' WORKSHEETS. WRITE EACH OF YOUR THREE INSPIRINGLY SMART DREAMS AT THE TOP OF EACH PAGE.

---

02 /

LIST AS MANY POTENTIAL BARRIERS TO YOU ACHIEVING EACH DREAM THAT YOU CAN THINK OF. REFER BACK TO MY EXPLANATION IF YOU NEED TO.

---

03 /

ONCE YOU'VE EXHAUSTED ALL THE IDEAS YOU HAVE ON BARRIERS, THEN – AND ONLY THEN – TURN YOUR ATTENTION TO POSSIBLE SOLUTIONS FOR EACH AND START WRITING. AGAIN, THIS IS A LIVING LIST. ADD TO IT WHENEVER YOU NEED TO.

---

04 /

UPDATE YOUR MASTER ACTION LISTS AS YOU UNCOVER MORE GREAT IDEAS FOR THINGS YOU NEED TO DO TO ACHIEVE YOUR DREAMS.

POTENTIAL BARRIERS AND POSSIBLE SOLUTIONS

1 IDENTIFYING BARRIERS –
BEFORE THEY BLOCK YOUR
PROGRESS – WILL HELP YOU
PROGRESS MUCH MORE QUICKLY

2 COMING UP WITH SOLUTIONS
TO ANY POTENTIAL PROBLEMS
WILL HELP INSPIRE YOU WITH
NEW IDEAS AND POSSIBLY NEW
THINGS TO DO TOO

PREPARING FOR THE IMPOSSIBLE DREAM

ALISA CAMPLIN-WARNER, OAM

first met Alisa Camplin-Warner on a plane from Sydney to Melbourne. Bright and bubbly, she'd struck up a conversation with my then seven-year-old son, Axel. 'She won an Olympic gold medal!' Axel blurted out as soon as Alisa was out of earshot.

Did she ever. It was maybe one of the most impossible gold medal wins in history, I later learnt, and an amazing example for us all of the power of dreaming, planning and overcoming obstacles.

Alisa was (and still is) incredibly passionate about sport. As a kid, she did athletics, gymnastics, hockey, sailing – you name it, she tried it – but those sports didn't work out. Alisa had a unique toolkit of skills and experience, but simply hadn't found the sport she loved yet.

Everything changed when she watched Australian aerial skier, Kirstie Marshall compete at the 1994 Lillehammer Winter Olympics. Then it dawned on Alisa that she had the strength, fortitude and acrobatic ability for aerial skiing ... she just needed to learn how to ski!

At nineteen years of age, Alisa had never even seen snow, let alone clipped into skis. But in that moment, she knew she'd found her sport, and her Olympic dream was ignited.

Determined to turn her dream into a reality, Alisa broke down her monumental goal into smaller, more manageable pieces. It was this goal planning that fuelled Alisa's self-belief and unlocked her dream of becoming an Olympic medallist.

Aerial skiing is without doubt one of the most challenging and dangerous of sports – athletes travel at speeds of 65 km/h, launching 40–50 feet into the air, to perform their acrobatic tricks. Alisa suffered numerous injuries along the way, including a broken collarbone, broken hand, separated shoulder, two broken ankles, multiple cracked ribs, a torn Achilles tendon, two knee reconstructions ... oh, and six concussions.

Another big challenge was finance. Aerial skiing is an expensive sport, so, while at university, Alisa worked several part-time jobs to pay for training at her nearest mountain (more than three hours' drive away), not to mention her lift tickets, travel and accommodation. She landed her first major sponsorship with a company in the lead up to the 2002 Salt Lake Olympics, but then another setback. Just six months before the Olympics, the company collapsed, leaving her in massive debt.

'From a young age, I loved sport, and I was good at it. The older I got, the more I wanted to know just how good I could be – I couldn't let money get in the way of achieving my dream! Worst case, I'd be pursuing something I loved and I'd discover my ultimate potential. To me, there was no real downside in chasing my dream, so I was determined to work harder and find a way.' And she did.

'I spent hours in the gym before work, did more jumps than anyone at the water ramps on the weekends and took private trampoline lessons after hours. I believe I did about 800 more training jumps into water than anyone else in the year before the Olympics.' And that was just the start...

'I practised to the sound of a full crowd so I wouldn't be daunted by noise on the day of competition. I trained after no food and without sleep, in case I was too nervous at the Olympics for either. I jumped with different equipment just in case something went wrong with mine. I hired a psychologist to ensure my mind was in the same peak condition as my body. I even ate the same breakfast for four years straight, because we tested it and I knew it was the right breakfast for me.'

And then a big setback. Alisa injured herself just a few weeks before the Olympics. At the time, she was told she had serious bone bruising. It wasn't until doctors examined her at Salt Lake that she discovered both ankles were fractured. The doctors were amazed that she was walking, let alone planning to jump. Alisa competed at the 2002 Olympics against doctors' advice. Can you imagine?

And all her pre-planning paid off in a big way. Alisa was so nervous the night before the final that she couldn't eat dinner. But she had prepared for that to happen. She struggled to get to sleep, but she knew she'd still be able to compete without sleep. Her dream came true when she landed a pair of triple-twisting double backflip jumps to win the event.

'To have landed the final jump and suddenly be on the other side of eight years of planning ... to see my name come up on the scoreboard as Olympic champion, there truly isn't a word to describe that moment. It was magic, disbelief, affirmation and relief all wrapped up in one,' she said.

The impossible dream had come true. A girl from Australia – a country known for its beaches and arid plains rather than its snow – had won gold.

What do you dream of but think is impossible? There's a chance you may be happily wrong.

Let Alisa's story inspire you to dream big – and reinforce how careful planning and focused action can help you make the impossible possible.

Take some time now while it's fresh in your mind to ponder on it and, in the space below, or in your Dream Life Journal, write down anything you've learnt that you could apply in your own life.

_____

_____

_____

_____

_____

_____

_____

_____

_____

_____

_____

_____

_____

THE GREATER THE OBSTACLE, THE

MORE GLORY IN OVERCOMING IT.

- MOLIÈRE -

CHAPTER TWENTY-TWO

WHAT SUPPORTS CAN I PUT IN PLACE?

YOUR DREAM LIFE STARTS HERE

WHAT SUPPORTS CAN I PUT IN PLACE?

This is another brilliant question to contemplate when you're in planning mode for a dream and you're making a long list of all the things you need to do.

But before you dive deeper into doing, now is a good time to remind you to keep looking at your dreams daily. Look at your Vision Board. Read your Dream Life Story. Do whatever you need to stay connected daily to your dreams and the reasons why they're important to you and your loved ones. Doing this is how you keep your motivation tank full and your energy high as you set about your doing.

You'll know from earlier in the book what I mean by supports, and it's well worth taking the time to focus purely on the question of what other supports you can put in place to ensure you reach your dream.

Using a simple example, if your dream is around exercise and sticking to a routine that you might find challenging, a simple support you could put in place could be to get your exercise clothes out and fill your water bottle the night before so you're ready to go from the moment you wake up.

Another support could be to book and pre-pay your exercise sessions so you don't have to think. You just need to show up. You've paid for it! Paying in advance is a great example of putting a support in place for those times when your motivation wanes or you have no cash at hand.

Putting supports in place is all about doing simple things to make it easier for you to do what you really need to do (a bit like going on autopilot). It may sound silly, but a great example of this for me was from years ago, in the wild start-up days of kikki.K, when I was constantly misplacing my keys. It drove me crazy. I wasted time looking for them. I got frustrated. And then I put one simple support in place and my problem of misplaced keys disappeared. I simply put a key hanger by the front door. A very simple support and so very effective.

Here's another example to help you get the hang of this exercise, using a big dream that one of our kikki.K lovers shared with me.

SUPPORTS I CAN PUT IN PLACE DREAM: 'TO BUY A BEACH HOUSE – WITHIN THE NEXT FIVE YEARS – THAT HAS A BEAUTIFUL VIEW AND WHERE WE CAN CREATE FAMILY MEMORIES FOR GENERATIONS TO COME.'	
POSSIBLE SUPPORT	**EXPLANATION**
HAVE A CLEAR BUDGET IN MIND AND PUT IN PLACE AN AUTOMATIC TRANSFER FROM OUR SALARIES INTO A BEACH HOUSE SAVINGS ACCOUNT.	AUTOMATES THE SAVINGS PROCESS.
SHARE THE DREAM WITH THE ENTIRE FAMILY. CREATE A VISION BOARD FOR EVERYONE TO CONTRIBUTE TO.	HELPS TO HAVE THE ENTIRE FAMILY ALIGNED AND EXCITED ABOUT WHAT WE NEED TO DO TO MAKE IT HAPPEN. HELPS US ACCEPT/WELCOME ANY TEMPORARY SACRIFICES FOR THE FAMILY IN THE CONTEXT OF ACHIEVING OUR FAMILY DREAM.
DECIDE ON POTENTIAL LOCATIONS AND GO AND MEET REAL ESTATE AGENTS IN THAT AREA.	GETS AGENTS INVOLVED IN SPOTTING PROPERTIES IN OUR BUDGET. STARTS TO MAKE IT ALL THE MORE REAL. ALSO HELPS BUILD UP OUR KNOWLEDGE OF THE MARKET.
DECIDE ON AND LOCK IN THE DIARY A PLAN TO TAKE SIMPLER/LESS EXPENSIVE ANNUAL HOLIDAYS FOR THE NEXT FIVE YEARS AND PUT WHAT WE SAVE INTO THE BEACH HOUSE SAVINGS ACCOUNT.	GIVES US SOMETHING TO LOOK FORWARD TO AND SUPPORTS OUR SAVINGS PLAN FOR OUR DREAM BEACH HOUSE.
TAKE TRIPS TO THE AREA WE LIKE. SPEND TIME WANDERING THE AREA, CHATTING TO LOCALS AND VISUALISING LIVING THERE.	THERE'S NOTHING LIKE VISUALISING HOW BEAUTIFUL IT WILL BE TO LIVE THERE TO HELP US DO WHAT WE NEED TO DO TO MAKE IT HAPPEN.
TAKE A PICTURE OF OUR FAVOURITE VIEW IN THAT AREA AND PUT IT ON THE WALL WHERE WE ALL SEE IT EVERY DAY.	SIMILAR TO ABOVE.

EXERCISE

IN YOUR DREAM LIFE JOURNAL:

01 /

GO TO THE 'SUPPORTS I CAN PUT IN PLACE' WORKSHEETS AND WRITE YOUR THREE INSPIRINGLY SMART DREAMS AT THE TOP OF THE PAGES.

---

02 /

LIST AS MANY IDEAS FOR SUPPORTS YOU CAN PUT IN PLACE TO HELP YOU ACHIEVE YOUR DREAM. REFER BACK TO MY EXPLANATION IF YOU NEED.

---

03 /

AGAIN, THIS IS A LIST THAT YOU CAN ADD TO WHENEVER YOU THINK OF SOMETHING NEW. JUST REMEMBER TO ADD ANY NEW ACTIONS TO YOUR MASTER ACTION LISTS.

SO, NOW WE'VE MADE SOME BIG PROGRESS – WELL DONE!

WHAT SUPPORTS CAN I PUT IN PLACE?

---

1 BUILDING A SUPPORT TEAM CAN KEEP YOUR MOTIVATION AND ENERGY LEVELS HIGH, EVEN WHEN THE GOING GETS TOUGH

---

2 DOING SIMPLE THINGS TO BUILD SUPPORTS INTO YOUR ROUTINE MAKES IT EASIER FOR YOU TO DO WHAT YOU REALLY NEED TO DO TO ACHIEVE YOUR DREAM

HOW I'VE APPLIED THESE 'DOING' PROCESSES

When I started out writing this book – a long-held dream – I brainstormed everything I could think of that I needed to do to make the book a reality. Before I began, I didn't really know where to start with that dream – it was so daunting. But getting all my ideas onto paper, even in a jumble at first, made it feel so much more achievable and exciting, and was a big leap forwards.

Then I asked myself, 'Who can help?' and wrote lists of all the people I needed to involve and how. For example, I knew nothing about publishing so I wrote lists of all the people I knew who had written books or who knew about publishing. From this, I created actions like, 'Have a coffee with Libby and listen to her experience with publishing options' and added those to my Master Action List.

Then I wrote a list of all of the potential barriers in my way and thought about how to overcome them. One of the potential barriers was limited time, so I spent a while going through my diary for the months ahead and arranged to put off other projects and commitments that weren't as important. This freed up time for the book, and I also had enough time to keep myself healthy and inspired along the way.

After that, I thought through what supports I needed to put in place. For example, I know I'm not so good with written English and knew I would need a lot of help with writing and editing my ideas, so I added, 'Think through and decide what support I need with writing' to my Master Action List too.

The list was long and varied. It included things like asking for advice from friends who'd distributed books, listening to useful podcasts on how to write a book, reflecting on everything I'd learnt about dreaming, gathering inspiration on how to design the book, writing a chapter plan, deciding on whether to self-publish or not ... oh, and making time in my diary over many weeks to actually write!

TO KEEP A LAMP BURNING WE HAVE

TO KEEP PUTTING OIL IN IT.

- MOTHER TERESA -

23

YOUR SEVEN KEY THINGS TO FOCUS ON

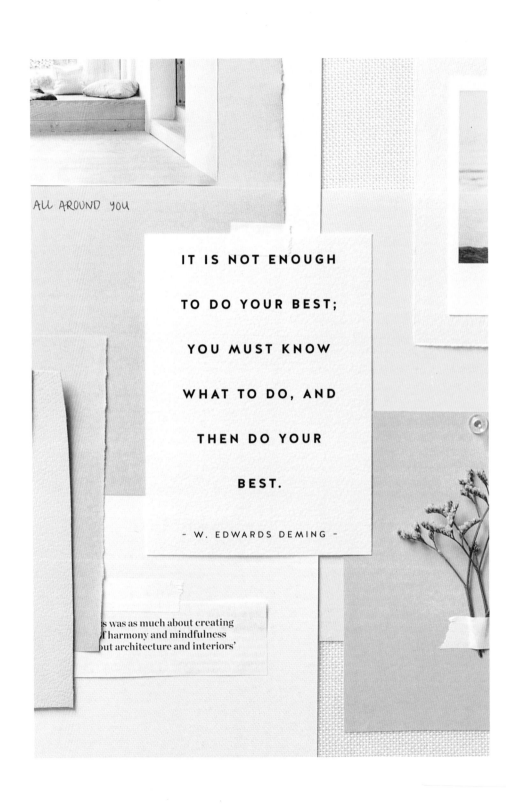

ALL AROUND YOU

IT IS NOT ENOUGH

TO DO YOUR BEST;

YOU MUST KNOW

WHAT TO DO, AND

THEN DO YOUR

BEST.

– W. EDWARDS DEMING –

s was as much about creating
f harmony and mindfulness
out architecture and interiors'

In the previous chapters, you've been building up your big long list of everything you'll need to do – all the actions required to bring your dream to life. Now, it's time to simplify. We need to identify what the absolutely most important seven things are for you to focus on.

I don't mean the first seven things. I mean, if you could ONLY do seven things to make the dream come true, what would they be? I find this to be a really powerful question. It seems so simple, but believe me, it's so worthwhile. Don't underestimate the traction this prioritised list will give you. Just go through your long list of actions, one by one, and ask yourself, 'Is this action *really* important enough to be in my top seven? If I could only do seven things to make my dream come true, would this be one of them?'

Why seven? My experience is that in chasing nearly any dream, there are no more than a few things that are absolutely crucial. Often it's only three or four, but I find that focusing on seven gives me a greater chance of uncovering the right three or four. Here's an example to help you get the idea. Using my dream of creating this book, the seven most important actions I selected from my long list were:

1. WRITE THE GUIDING BRIEF AND CHAPTER PLAN FOR THE BOOK.
2. DECIDE ON WHO I NEED TO JOIN ME IN MAKING THE BOOK A REALITY AND ASSIGN CLEAR ROLES AND RESPONSIBILITIES.
3. DECIDE ON WHETHER TO SELF-PUBLISH OR NOT.
4. CREATE A PROJECT PLAN WITH KEY MILESTONES AND KEY DATES – INCLUDING REGULAR QUICK MEETINGS TO KEEP US ON TRACK AND ALIGNED – AND SHARE THIS WITH THE TEAM (UPDATE AS NECESSARY).
5. BOOK TIME IN MY CALENDAR FOR ALL THE THINGS I NEED TO DO TO MAKE THE PROJECT HAPPEN – AND DECIDE ON WHAT OTHER ACTIVITIES TO POSTPONE.
6. MAKE SURE THERE IS PLENTY OF TIME BUILT INTO THE SCHEDULE TO ALLOW ME TO REVIEW AND REFLECT ON PROGRESS SO THE BOOK CONTENT IS AS INSPIRING, EMPOWERING AND SIMPLE AS IT CAN BE.
7. BUILD IN TIME FOR ME TO FEEL BALANCED (FAMILY, PERSONAL AND WORK), HEALTHY AND INSPIRED DURING THE PROCESS.

There were so many other actions I needed to do, but these seven were the most important and that's where I started.

A PERSON WHO CAN

CREATE IDEAS WORTHY

OF NOTE IS A PERSON

WHO HAS LEARNED

MUCH FROM OTHERS.

- KONOSUKE MATSUSHITA -

IN YOUR DREAM LIFE JOURNAL:

01 /

SELECT THE TOP SEVEN ACTIONS THAT YOU WILL NEED TO TAKE TO MAKE YOUR DREAM REAL. REFER BACK TO MY EXPLANATION ON PAGE 301 IF YOU NEED TO. TAKE YOUR TIME – THESE ARE SOME OF THE MOST IMPORTANT DECISIONS YOU'LL MAKE AS YOU CHASE YOUR DREAM.

02 /

WRITE THEM DOWN IN ORDER OF THEIR IMPORTANCE AS YOU SEE IT, WITH 1 AS THE HIGHEST IMPORTANCE AND 7 THE LOWEST. REPEAT FOR YOUR OTHER TWO DREAMS. WHAT TO DO WITH EVERYTHING ELSE ON YOUR LONG ACTION LISTS? WE'LL GET TO THAT SOON.

YOUR SEVEN KEY THINGS TO FOCUS ON

1 CHOOSING JUST A FEW REALLY IMPORTANT ACTIONS TO FOCUS ON WILL GIVE YOU CLARITY AND STOP YOU GETTING OVERWHELMED

2 FOCUSING ON WHAT YOU ABSOLUTELY MUST DO WILL MOVE YOU AHEAD MORE QUICKLY AND HELP KEEP YOU INSPIRED AS YOU SEE THE PROGRESS YOU MAKE

3 DON'T UNDERESTIMATE THE TRACTION THIS PRIORITISED LIST WILL GIVE YOU

CHAPTER TWENTY-FOUR

CREATING YOUR ONE-PAGE DREAM ROADMAP

YOUR DREAM LIFE STARTS HERE

Now, just as you did with each of your three top dreams, it's important to make your seven key actions SMART too – resulting in a clear, specific and realistic step-by-step Dream Roadmap to follow for each dream. Keep it simple, but make sure that the seven critical things you need to do to achieve each dream are SMART.

As you do this, it's a great chance to spend some time challenging yourself on how you can get these seven key things done in the most efficient, effective way.

I find it really valuable to ask myself: 'How can I get them done with the least possible effort?'

THERE IS ALWAYS MORE THAN ONE WAY TO GET ANYTHING DONE.

Let me share an example (you'll no doubt have many of your own). It had been a long-held dream of mine to have my beautiful kikki.K products sold via the high quality, US-based Nordstrom department stores. I'd read a lot about their approach to service and fashion, their history as a Swedish family who'd immigrated to the US, and I shopped their stores, respected their vision and felt the fit was perfect.

There are so many ways I could have attempted to meet with someone at Nordstrom. I wrote a big long list of things I could do, including emailing a buyer or calling their head office receptionist and asking to be put through to the right person. I reminded myself to focus on finding the absolutely key things I needed to do and that there is always more than one way to get anything done.

Asking myself: 'How can I do this with the least possible effort?' and 'Who can help me?', I hit on a much better idea. I asked any of my friends who may have had business dealings with Nordstrom if they knew anyone who worked there and, if yes, could they give me a warm introduction.

It turned out that one of my friends knew Pete Nordstrom, Co-President of Nordstrom, and she was delighted to introduce us. I met with Pete and shared how I felt kikki.K could help them meet the needs of their customers. To cut a long story short, we're now stocked in Nordstrom's beautiful stores. It was a dream come true – and all strongly influenced by me trying to find a better way to get something done.

This just goes to show how doors can be opened for you by talking to people and actively seeking connections that could inch you closer to the end result – and particularly by asking yourself: 'How can I get this done with the least possible effort?'

Think hard about your seven key actions and how you can get them done in the simplest, most effective way. Now back to the process...

Estimate how long each key action will take, choose a start date and a completion deadline, break them down into smaller tasks if necessary and think through who can help with each (if anyone).

Once that's all done – even in rough form – I find it a good idea to run it by someone I respect (preferably someone who's achieved what I am setting out to do) and ask them what they think of my plan. In years gone by, I've sometimes also done this with a mentor or with a coach.

Remember the question, 'Who?' Maybe, just maybe, there's someone around with more experience than you who can radically improve the way you approach getting these seven things done so it's quicker and easier for you to achieve your dream. It's definitely worth you spending some time thinking about just that.

It doesn't matter if you don't have access to a mentor – it's not a necessity, but bouncing your plan for achieving your dream off the right people can be so profoundly powerful. As you talk it through with them, you'll often see it from a different perspective and new ideas about what needs to be done – and what doesn't – will emerge.

After doing this myself, I've often walked away with clarity and with solutions that seemed so simple afterwards. You'll find that too when you talk with people who have deep experience in doing what you want to do. Just remember my caution about seeking input from people who do not have personal experience in achieving your dream, as they may send you down the wrong path.

Right now, these are your most important seven actions and you never know – you just might find ways of getting them done that weren't obvious before. If you do, update your Master Action List as needed.

Here's an example:

MY DREAM: TO BE THE FITTEST I HAVE EVER BEEN

AS AN INSPIRINGLY SMART DREAM:

IT'S THE 7TH OF FEBRUARY 2019, I'M THE FITTEST I'VE EVER BEEN BY MY THREE KEY MEASURES. I FEEL STRONG, HEALTHY, PROUD AND ENERGISED BECAUSE OF IT AND HAVE DEVELOPED ALL OF THE HABITS AND SUPPORT SYSTEMS I NEED TO STAY THAT WAY.

MY TOP SEVEN ACTIONS MADE SMART:

+ RESEARCH GYMS/CLASSES AND CREATE A SCHEDULE FOR ALL MY EXERCISES IN MY DIARY BY [DATE]
+ SEE A NATUROPATH – AND SEE IF I'M LOW ON ANYTHING – TO SUPPORT MY FITNESS PLAN BY [DATE]
+ DECIDE WHETHER TO HAVE A PT/FITNESS COACH OR NOT BY [DATE]
+ DECIDE ON THE THREE KEY MEASURES OF PROGRESS BY [DATE]
+ PUT UP MY DREAM ON THE BATHROOM MIRROR AND A CHART TO TICK OFF DAILY WHEN DONE BY [DATE]
+ CREATE A FITNESS VISION BOARD AND PUT ON WALL BY [DATE]
+ SET UP A GROUP OF FRIENDS TO BE ACCOUNTABLE TO BY [DATE]

Once you have clarity on everything involved in getting those seven key actions done and you've made each of them SMART, put them in your diary. This is one of the simplest but most important things you will ever do. And make sure your deadlines are realistic – by this, I mean give yourself plenty of time around all the other commitments in your life.

As you do this, you'll start to create a really simple plan that guides you to do what you need to do and when. You won't need to waste any mental energy wondering if you've forgotten something – it's all there in front of you in your diary. All you need to do is just do it!

Now I know life often throws up things that get in the way and may end up taking priority over actions you've set yourself to achieve your dream. That's normal and okay. If you want your dream enough, you'll find a way to adjust your plan when you need to.

You've now built good momentum, have a plan developing and you're setting yourself up to see your dream come to life. You've worked out what the seven most important things are to focus on – *and* you've put them in your diary. Great start.

So what should you do with the many other actions you've brainstormed? Simply follow the same process you've been through with your top seven actions.

If you carry out each action, you will eventually achieve your dream. Keep reminding yourself of the reason WHY you are chasing your dream. Looking at your Vision Board or Vision Book daily will help inspire you, as will reading your Dream Life Story regularly.

Congratulations you! What you have now done – after completing the above – is create a Dream Roadmap for each of your important dreams and a diarised plan of action to follow as you take your dreams from your beautiful heart-driven imaginings to something that is very real and very doable.

You are on your way – with a clear path ahead. I'm so excited for you.

LET'S TAKE ACTION:

01 /

ON THE DREAM ROADMAPS IN YOUR DREAM LIFE JOURNAL, REWRITE EACH OF THE THREE DREAMS YOU ARE CHASING AT THE TOP OF THREE SEPARATE PAGES, THEN REWRITE THE SEVEN KEY ACTIONS FOR EACH MAKING THEM ALL SMART. BE SURE TO CHOOSE A START AND COMPLETION DATE FOR EACH, BREAK THEM DOWN INTO SMALLER TASKS IF NECESSARY AND THINK THROUGH WHO CAN HELP WITH EACH (IF ANYONE). IF YOU NEED TO, REFER BACK TO THE DIRECTIONS ON THE SMART CONCEPT IN CHAPTER 18.

NOW YOU HAVE A SIMPLE OVERVIEW OF ALL THE KEY THINGS YOU NEED TO DO AND WHEN. KEEP IT HANDY.

02 /

ONCE YOU'VE DONE THAT WORK, CONSIDER BOUNCING YOUR ROADMAP FOR EACH OF YOUR DREAMS OFF SOMEONE WHO HAS EXPERIENCE IN WHAT YOU WANT TO ACHIEVE. UPDATE YOUR ROADMAP WITH THEIR INPUT IF NECESSARY.

03 /

PUT THE KEY DATES AND TASKS IN YOUR DIARY, AND ON THE DAY YOU COME ACROSS EACH ACTION IN YOUR DIARY, DO IT! THEY'RE IMPORTANT TO YOU.

04 /

IF IT FEELS RIGHT FOR YOU GIVEN YOUR PERSONAL CIRCUMSTANCES, SHARE YOUR THREE ONE-PAGE DREAM ROADMAPS WITH US AND OUR COMMUNITY OF DREAMERS BY TAKING PHOTOS OF THEM AND SHARING THEM VIA @KRISTINAKIKKIK AND @KIKKI.K - USING #KIKKIKDREAMLIFE AND #101MILLIONDREAMERS. HOPEFULLY EITHER I, OR SOMEONE IN OUR COMMUNITY, WILL GET THE CHANCE TO COMMENT WITH ANY THOUGHTS THAT COULD HELP YOU ACHIEVE THEM. WE'D LOVE TO HEAR FROM YOU WHEN YOU ACHIEVE THESE DREAMS, SO KEEP SHARING YOUR SUCCESSES AND ANY KEY LEARNINGS WITH US ALL TOO. WE CAN ALL LEARN FROM AND INSPIRE EACH OTHER.

05 /

NOW YOU JUST HAVE TO REVISIT THE LONG LIST OF ACTIONS ON YOUR MASTER ACTION LISTS THAT DIDN'T MAKE YOUR TOP SEVEN AND FOLLOW THE SAME PROCESS YOU'VE BEEN THROUGH ABOVE TO MAKE EACH SMART AND SCHEDULE THEM INTO YOUR DIARY.

CREATING YOUR ONE-PAGE DREAM ROADMAP

1 NOW THAT YOU HAVE YOUR KEY THINGS TO FOCUS ON, MAKE SURE EACH IS CLEAR AND ACTIONABLE FOR YOU

2 SPEND SOME TIME CHALLENGING YOURSELF ON HOW YOU CAN GET THESE SEVEN KEY THINGS DONE IN THE MOST EFFICIENT, EFFECTIVE WAY

3 CONSIDER BOUNCING YOUR PLAN OFF A PERSON OR PEOPLE WHO HAVE DEEP EXPERIENCE IN WHAT YOU WANT TO DO

4 PUT KEY ACTIONS IN YOUR DIARY – AND COMMIT TO DOING THEM

5 KEEP YOUR ONE-PAGE DREAM ROADMAPS WHERE YOU'LL SEE THEM DAILY

25

DREAMING – IT'S A LIFELONG PROCESS

YOUR DREAM LIFE STARTS HERE

When I was younger I thought I would arrive at some point in the future where I was grown up and felt completely satisfied with my life. That never happened! Now I'm so glad this isn't the case because I love growing and evolving.

Sometimes I pinch myself and feel so content that I'm living my dream life, but in many ways, I honestly feel like I'm just getting started and I think that's wonderful too. The chance to empower and inspire people around the world to create their dream lives is so exciting for me.

Like mine, *your* dreams will change as you grow and change as a person. I want you to know that it's okay to let go of some dreams if they no longer feel right. That's the best thing about life – we evolve and our dreams evolve too. For that very reason, it's important to have a process where you check in with your dreams regularly, so you can review them and make sure you're on track or update them if you need to. Dreaming is a lifelong process.

As you now know, I like to reflect and set new dreams and then goals at the end of every year, to set myself up for the year ahead. You can start at any time though – remember, the most important thing is just to start. I set dreams and goals annually and then I like to work to a quarterly rhythm.

Every three months, I check in with my dreams and review where I'm at, then I set new priorities for the next quarter. I'll set different priorities for each month, but I always know that I have time set aside each week and most days to work on them. Life gets busy, so if you don't lock in that time to begin with, it will always get filled with other tasks.

Now, this dreaming rhythm that I follow might not be right for you, particularly if you're just getting started, so take time to think about what is achievable for you.

Right now, I'd love you to contemplate and decide on an annual dreaming rhythm that you can commit to, then schedule that in to your diary or calendar, keeping in mind that while reading this book and doing the exercises you have likely diarised specific exercises and started creating an annual rhythm for yourself already.

Things you'll need to consider include: Will you set new dreams each year? What feels right for you? Will it help you as part of your dreaming rhythm to review your dreams with a supportive and inspiring friend or group of people who can help you get clear on your top priorities, or do you prefer to spend time alone to figure it all out?

I recommend that every year you re-read this book and redo all of the exercises. Choose the best month for you to do this and diarise the time you need for that.

Following is an overview of what I recommend. Use it to decide on the rhythm that works best for you – and, like the rest of the process, review that rhythm over time and adjust it as needed.

Once you set your rhythm in place – and you diarise it all – stick to that like you would any other important meeting or appointment. This is your time for your dreams so that you can live your dream life. It's so important. I can't wait to see what you do with your power. Enjoy it.

ACTIONS

DAILY / WEEKLY

- CULTIVATE AN OPENNESS TO THE PRACTICE OF DREAMING AND WRITING DOWN DREAMS AS THEY COME TO YOU. KEEP YOUR 101 DREAMS LIST CLOSE SO YOU CAN ADD TO IT WHENEVER YOU COME UP WITH A NEW DREAM YOU THINK YOU MIGHT WANT TO CHASE. YOU MAY WANT TO USE YOUR DREAM LIFE BLUEPRINT INSTEAD (CHAPTER 12) AND PUT DREAMS DIRECTLY INTO THE LIFE AREA YOU FEEL IS MOST RELEVANT. IT'S UP TO YOU.

- CULTIVATE A HABIT OF ASKING OTHERS ABOUT THEIR DREAMS AND BEING INSPIRED.

- KEEP YOUR LIST OF PEOPLE YOU WANT TO MEET CLOSE SO YOU CAN ADD TO IT WHENEVER YOU COME UP WITH A NEW PERSON YOU THINK YOU MAY WANT TO MEET.

- LOOK AT YOUR VISION BOARD AND/OR VISION BOOK DAILY.

- BE OPEN TO SHARING YOUR DREAMS WITH THE RIGHT PEOPLE.

ACTIONS

+ DO THE POWERFUL 101 DREAMS EXERCISE AS OFTEN AS YOU LIKE OVER THE COURSE OF YOUR
  YEAR AND LIFE. I'D SUGGEST DOING IT EVERY THREE MONTHS, BUT DO IT AT LEAST ANNUALLY.

+ I SUGGEST DOING THE POWERFUL 'LIST OF PEOPLE YOU'D LOVE TO MEET' EXERCISE EVERY
  THREE MONTHS, BUT DO IT AT LEAST ANNUALLY.

+ IF IT'S SOMETHING YOU FEEL COMFORTABLE WITH, I'D SUGGEST CREATING YOUR OWN
  DREAM GROUP AND MEETING EVERY FEW MONTHS.

+ REVIEW THE WORK YOU DID IN THE 'DREAMING' EXERCISES IN CHAPTERS 4–17.

+ REVIEW YOUR TOP DREAMS AGAINST THE 'DOING' EXERCISES IN CHAPTERS 18–24 EVERY
  THREE MONTHS (OR MORE FREQUENTLY AS NEEDED).

RE-READ THIS BOOK AND REDO ALL THE EXERCISES

+ CHOOSE THE BEST MONTH FOR YOU TO DO THIS AND SCHEDULE TIME IN YOUR DIARY. NEAR
  THE START OF A NEW CALENDAR YEAR WORKS WELL FOR MANY PEOPLE I KNOW. ONCE
  YOU'VE READ THE BOOK AND DONE THE EXERCISES ONCE, YOU'LL GET THROUGH IT ALL MUCH
  MORE QUICKLY EACH YEAR AS YOU BUILD FAMILIARITY WITH THE CONTENT AND PROCESS.

IF NOT DOING THAT, AT LEAST DO THE FOLLOWING:

+ REDO THE POWERFUL 101 DREAMS EXERCISE.

+ REVISIT THE 'LIST OF PEOPLE YOU'D LOVE TO MEET' EXERCISE.

+ IF YOU'VE CREATED YOUR OWN DREAM GROUP, ORGANISE AN ANNUAL CATCH-UP (OF
  COURSE, YOU MAY BE MEETING MUCH MORE FREQUENTLY).

+ DO THE 'WHO ARE YOU AND WHERE ARE YOU AT RIGHT NOW?' EXERCISES – A BIT LIKE AN
  ANNUAL HEALTH CHECK. I USUALLY DO THESE IN NOVEMBER OR DECEMBER WHEN I'M STARTING
  TO SET GOALS AND PLAN FOR THE NEW YEAR, BUT YOU CAN DO IT WHENEVER YOU CHOOSE.

+ REDO THE EXERCISES IN CHAPTER 12 (START PULLING IT TOGETHER) AND CHAPTER 13
  (VISUALISE – WRITE YOUR DREAM LIFE STORY). DO THESE POWERFUL EXERCISES AS OFTEN
  AS YOU LIKE OVER THE COURSE OF YOUR LIFE – AT LEAST ANNUALLY.

+ FULL REVIEW OF YOUR KEY DREAMS AND HOW TO ACHIEVE THEM WITH THE 'DOING'
  EXERCISES IN CHAPTERS 18–24.

+ REVIEW YOUR DREAMING RHYTHM.

EXERCISE

01 /

IN YOUR DREAM LIFE JOURNAL, REFLECT ON YOUR JOURNEY NOW THAT YOU'VE REACHED THE END
OF THIS BOOK. TAKE A MOMENT TO CONSIDER HOW YOU FEEL. WHAT ARE YOU LOOKING FORWARD
TO? WHAT WILL THE CHALLENGES BE? AND HOW WILL YOU OVERCOME THEM?

_____

02 /

SET ASIDE TIME EACH WEEK TO WORK ON YOUR DREAMS AND TOP PRIORITIES - DO NOT SKIP THIS!

_____

03 /

CONSIDER MY RECOMMENDED DREAMING RHYTHM AND DECIDE WHAT WILL WORK FOR YOU.
REFLECT ON ALL OF THE EXERCISES YOU'VE DONE IN THE BOOK THAT YOU WANT TO DO ON
A REGULAR BASIS AND BUILD THEM INTO YOUR DAY.

_____

04 /

FROM THE MOMENT YOU BEGIN THIS PROCESS, CONTINUE TO REASSESS AND READJUST SO THAT
IT WORKS BEST WITH YOUR LIFE. ONCE A YEAR, RE-READ THIS BOOK AND REDO THE EXERCISES -
YOU'LL BE AMAZED AT HOW YOUR DREAMS WILL EVOLVE AND CHANGE OVER TIME. MARK TIME FOR
THAT IN YOUR DIARY NOW.

_____

05 /

START TODAY!

DREAMING - IT'S A LIFELONG PROCESS

1 YOUR DREAMS AND GOALS WILL CHANGE OVER TIME AS YOU GROW AND CHANGE AS A PERSON

2 DON'T BE AFRAID TO LET GO OF DREAMS THAT AREN'T SERVING YOU WELL ANYMORE

3 SETTING UP A REGULAR RHYTHM FOR THE YEAR AHEAD IN YOUR DIARY FOR DREAMING AND OTHER RELATED PRACTICES ENSURES YOU WILL PRIORITISE THE SPACE AND TIME YOU NEED TO THINK BIG AND FOCUS ON CREATING YOUR DREAM LIFE

WHAT YOU DO EVERY DAY

MATTERS MORE THAN WHAT

YOU DO ONCE IN A WHILE.

- GRETCHEN RUBIN -

WHAT NOW?

'IF YOU ARE WORKING ON SOMETHING EXCITING
THAT YOU REALLY CARE ABOUT, YOU DON'T HAVE
TO BE PUSHED. THE VISION PULLS YOU.'

- STEVE JOBS -

SHARE YOUR DREAMS AND ACHIEVEMENTS WITH ME
AND INSPIRE OTHERS...

Y ou read earlier that my biggest dream is to inspire and empower 101 million people around the world to put three dreams in writing and create seven key actions for achieving each dream.

I'm so passionate about this. I know we can create a profoundly positive impact and send waves of change and inspiration around the world this way. Please join in the conversation with me and with our global community of like-minded dreamers by following and sharing via @kristinakikkik and @kikki.K – using #kikkiKDreamLife and #101MillionDreamers.

Connect more deeply and learn more at www.kikki-k.com/dreamlife...

At the time of writing, we're hard at work building a portal for you and our global online dream community. This will have a curated selection of inspiration, tools, content and products for you, and a range of simple and practical e-learning courses to provide ongoing support for you on your journey.

Visit www.kikki-k.com/dreamlife to find out more up-to-date information and to register your interest so we can let you know when anything new is released that could be valuable for you.

Subscribe to my podcast and blog...

If you liked the inspiring stories from the amazing people in the book like Dr Tererai Trent, Arianna and others, be sure to subscribe to my podcasts and blog for more inspiring interviews and content via www.kikki-k.com/dreamlife.

Inspire others to dream...

And if you've found this book and process valuable, help send waves of possibility around the globe by recommending or gifting a copy of this book and a Dream Life Journal to anyone you know who'll benefit.

And of course, you can find more inspiration, tools, content and products to inspire you to continue living your dream life at kikki-k.com.

IF YOU REALLY WANT

SOMETHING YOU CAN

FIGURE OUT HOW TO

MAKE IT HAPPEN.

- CHER -

THE OFTEN UNEXPECTED POWER OF DREAMING

When I started writing this book, I had a few groups of people in mind that I thought would benefit from my stories, learnings and experiences. I kept them in mind as I wrote.

These were various groups of people. Girls I know who are young and just starting to think about what they wanted to do with their lives. The many people I've met during my talks across the globe – ranging from the inspired and energised who are chasing great dreams to the way-too-many people who tell me they're unhappy with their career or something else in their lives. Some who want to start businesses combining their passions and values. Others who simply want to get more from their family life, work or creative pursuits.

But one group in particular that kept surfacing in my mind as I wrote was my own book group – a diverse range of wonderful, high-achieving women from various walks of life. When I spend time with them, I always feel I can do anything. They are ambitious, bold, curious and fun. And they are all into self-improvement and personal development. Most of them have their own successful businesses and are taking on the world.

As I was in the early stages of writing, I kept asking myself, 'would my book group benefit from this book?' – knowing how each month we devour a book, analyse it, discuss it and look for nuggets of gold that will benefit our lives. And I kept coming back to the same answer. And the answer was, 'maybe not?'

I felt they were already dreaming so big and so boldly that dreaming was not something they needed much help with.

Over time those thoughts nagged at me – maybe you can relate to when something keeps playing on your mind, usually for a good reason. I started thinking, 'I love dreaming and I find the practice and process I've refined so valuable. Simple steps repeated often. So maybe they will too?'

EVENTUALLY, DEEPER INTO WRITING THE BOOK AND STILL UNCERTAIN,
I DECIDED I NEEDED TO KNOW THE ANSWER.

On impulse, as I was setting the dinner table for our monthly book group gathering – it was my turn to host – I included a kikki.K Dreams Journal as part of the table setting for each of the members. The soft pink journals matched with pink roses, candles and a white tablecloth. It was the perfect setting for some dreaming.

So over dinner and a discussion of the book we'd all read, I suggested I could guide them through a 101 Dreams session – essentially the key exercise from the first chapter in this book. The result was amazing.

This group, who I'd thought might not need the practice of dreaming, was so inspired by it!

They imagined, reimagined, created and discovered some amazing dreams for themselves that night. Some small and some big. All from the heart. They were no different to anyone else I'd guided through the dreaming practice. It was a relief in some ways and a very exciting validation of the power of dreaming for anyone.

It was such a wonderful night and, as everyone around the table shared their new dreams, we all took inspiration from each other.

But it's something else that came out of this story that I really want to share with you – which beautifully illustrates how sharing your dreams can lead to amazing and unexpected outcomes...

I was in Sydney a few days later and went for a beautiful early morning walk around Bondi Beach with one of my closest friends and fellow book group member, Anna-Carin. She shared with me that she had been so inspired by the dreaming exercise at our recent dinner that she was going to guide her entrepreneurs' group through the same exercise that afternoon. Later that night, inspired by the dreaming session, Anna-Carin messaged me, sharing with me what she said was an inspiring podcast about dreaming. That podcast was to become life changing for me...

The podcast was called *The School of Greatness* with Lewis Howes. And the first episode was called 'Awaken to Your Full Potential and Achieve the Impossible' – an interview with the amazing Dr Tererai Trent, a woman whose name I did not know.

I read in the summary that Tererai had been chosen by Oprah Winfrey as her 'all-time favourite guest' from tens of thousands of guests on thousands of Oprah's shows. That was enough to get my attention, so I decided I had to listen to it straight away, even if it was late at night.

And Tererai's story was remarkable.

I hung off every word. My heart raced. I cried. I rejoiced at the beauty of the human spirit – and I marvelled at how she had been inspired to write down her dreams on paper, to chase them and, seemingly miraculously, to achieve them. I was stunned by what she had achieved – for herself and for the betterment of her community – all because someone gave her permission to dream. That part of her story was so much like my own 3am moment.

Being in the middle of writing my book on the power of dreaming, her story was a bolt of inspiration. It showcased nearly every important thing that I had learned and wanted to share with the world via my book.

I was so very inspired, and I felt everything was coming together. You know that feeling when you feel that things are happening for a reason?

'I have to share her story in my book,' was my first thought. 'It will be so incredibly inspiring for people.' Tererai had what seemed like impossible dreams, but after hearing her story, nothing seemed impossible.

And more than that, her story had such an impact on me that I had an overwhelming urge to find a way to help her achieve her new dreams, to bring education to generations of children otherwise denied an education. I decided I just had to get in touch with her.

So, I reached out to her, and that was the start of our partnership – which only came about as a result of dreaming with my book group.

The first time we met was on a video call. She was in New Mexico in the United States and I was in Melbourne. Her image came up on the screen and the first impression I had was of how young she looked. I spent the first ten minutes smiling inexplicably. It was such a privilege to hear her story and new dreams firsthand after all I'd read about her.

It was simply amazing to see and feel her fire and passion, knowing where she had come from and what she had achieved – from a young, poor, uneducated girl to a woman who addressed the UN Global Leaders Summit in 2013 with a powerful voice and meaningful message, and received a standing ovation. Knowing that she has directly influenced the lives of thousands of children and indirectly hundreds of thousands – probably millions – more, as Oprah and others have shared her story around the world. Knowing that children of hers were now at university and that, in one generation, her dreams and actions had broken the cycle of poverty and lack of access to education that had been her family's past.

EPILOGUE

Words can hardly describe the feeling of being in the presence of someone who has done all that yet describes herself as 'just a girl from a tiny village in Zimbabwe'.

It was so very inspiring, heartwarming and humbling – and her genuine warmth made me feel like I'd found a long-lost sister.

We've since decided to collaborate by sharing her story in this book and donating US$1 from every book sold to the Tererai Trent International Foundation.

Tererai will also join me on a global speaking tour to promote the book and the movement we are building to inspire and empower 101 million people across the world to write down three dreams on paper and start chasing them, giving Tererai a platform to share her story and her new dreams with a large international audience. We're also making plans to collaborate on a product range that will build a sustainable income to help fund her important work, and we have many other similar exciting initiatives under development.

Isn't it just amazing that the two of us – from such different backgrounds – have been brought together by the power of dreaming? A Swede and a Zimbabwean. An entrepreneur and a humanitarian. One who had the privilege of education as a child and one who did not. Both lives influenced so profoundly by someone giving them permission to dream – by writing those dreams down on paper and then chasing them.

Together we will do amazing things to inspire the world to dream – and do!

As Tererai would say, '*Tinogona* – it is achievable!'

Where will dreaming take you?

YOUR DREAM READING AND RESOURCE LIST

+ BERESFORD, BRUCE, DIR. *MAO'S LAST DANCER*. 2009; PADDINGTON, NSW: GREAT SCOTT PRODUCTIONS, FILM.

+ BRANSON, RICHARD. *FINDING MY VIRGINITY: A NEW AUTOBIOGRAPHY*. LONDON: PORTFOLIO PUBLISHING, 2017.

+ CAMPLIN-WARNER, ALISA. *HIGH FLYER*. MELBOURNE: LOTHIAN BOOKS, 2005.

+ CUNXIN, LI. *MAO'S LAST DANCER*. MELBOURNE: PENGUIN VIKING, 2003.

+ CUNXIN, LI. *THE PEASANT PRINCE*. MELBOURNE: PENGUIN VIKING, 2007.

+ DEMARTINI, JOHN. 'DEMARTINI VALUE DETERMINATION.' DRDEMARTINI.COM. 2018. HTTPS://DRDEMARTINI.COM/VALUE_DETERMINATION/DETERMINE_YOUR_VALUES

+ FERRISS, TIMOTHY. *THE 4-HOUR WORK WEEK*. NEW YORK: HARMONY BOOKS, 2007.

+ HUFFINGTON, ARIANNA. *THRIVE: THE THIRD METRIC TO REDEFINING SUCCESS AND CREATING A LIFE OF WELL-BEING, WISDOM, AND WONDER*. NEW YORK: HARMONY BOOKS, 2014.

+ JEFFERS, SUSAN. *FEEL THE FEAR AND DO IT ANYWAY*. NEW YORK: BALLANTINE BOOKS, 1987.

+ LEMKE, LISA. *THE SUMMER TABLE*. NEW YORK: STERLING EPICURE, 2015.

+ LEMKE, LISA. *THE WINTER TABLE*. NEW YORK: STERLING EPICURE, 2017.

+ OPRAH WINFREY NETWORK. 'OPRAH SURPRISES TERERAI TRENT.' YOUTUBE VIDEO, 4:08. NOVEMBER 11, 2011. HTTPS://WWW.YOUTUBE.COM/WATCH?V=NQWABHF45QI

+ SCHWARTZ, DAVID. *THE MAGIC OF THINKING BIG*. NEW JERSEY: PRENTICE HALL, 1959.

+ SHARMA, ROBIN. *LEADERSHIP WISDOM FROM THE MONK WHO SOLD HIS FERRARI*. NEW YORK: HARPERCOLLINS PUBLISHERS, 2010.

+ TEDX TALKS. 'FORGOTTEN WOMEN AND GIRLS – TERERAI TRENT.' YOUTUBE VIDEO, 19:12. NOVEMBER 4, 2015. HTTPS://WWW.YOUTUBE.COM/WATCH?V=2N2DXFHWTE4

+ TERERAI TRENT. 'DR TERERAI TRENT OPENING THE UN GLOBAL LEADERS SUMMIT NYC.' YOUTUBE VIDEO, 11:07. APRIL 24, 2014. HTTPS://WWW.YOUTUBE.COM/WATCH?V=X1M9LX-D87C

+ TRENT, TERERAI. *THE AWAKENED WOMAN: A GUIDE FOR REMEMBERING & REIGNITING YOUR SACRED DREAMS*. NEW YORK: ATRIA/ENLIVEN BOOKS, 2017.

+ TRENT, TERERAI. *THE GIRL WHO BURIED HER DREAMS IN A CAN: A TRUE STORY*. NEW YORK: PENGUIN PUTNAM INC, 2016.

+ WARE, BRONNIE. *THE TOP FIVE REGRETS OF THE DYING: A LIFE TRANSFORMED BY THE DEARLY DEPARTING*. CARLSBAD, CA: HAY HOUSE, 2012.

+ WINFREY, OPRAH. *THE WISDOM OF SUNDAYS: LIFE-CHANGING INSIGHTS FROM SUPER SOUL CONVERSATIONS*. NEW YORK: FLATIRON BOOK, 2017.

MORE THANKS

THERE ARE SO MANY PEOPLE I WANT TO THANK...
THOSE WHO WORKED SPECIFICALLY ON THIS PROJECT WITH ME –
JENNIFER, FRAN, DOMINI, VICTORIA H, VICTORIA K, STEPH, IRENA AND TARIN.
MY PROOFREADERS AND TEST DREAMERS – KATIE, BEN,
ANDREA, IAIN, LILLIAN L, MARK AND LILLIAN O.

...AND OTHERS WHO HAVE MADE THE WHOLE JOURNEY POSSIBLE:

ALLEYNE LACY (PAUL'S MOTHER) – THANK YOU FOR YOUR NEVER-ENDING
MORAL SUPPORT AND FOR BELIEVING IN US SO MUCH THAT YOU
MORTGAGED YOUR HOME FOR MANY YEARS TO HELP US
FINANCE THE BUSINESS. NEVER FORGOTTEN.

MY MOTHER AND FATHER EIVOR AND INGVAR KARLSSON – THANK YOU FOR
THE VALUES YOU INSTILLED IN ME, AND YOUR SUPPORT IN SO MANY WAYS.

TODD TREVAKS – A RETAIL ADVISOR AND DEAR MAN
WHO BELIEVED IN ME FROM THE EARLY DAYS.

GILLIAN FRANKLIN AND GRAEME WISE – THANK YOU SO MUCH FOR THE
MANY MENTORING CONVERSATIONS AS WE WERE STARTING OUT, FROM
WHICH I WALKED OUT AT LEAST A FOOT TALLER THAN I WALKED IN.

ANNA-CARIN – WHO RAN SHOP NUMBER THREE
AND HAS BEEN INVOLVED IN SO MUCH.

PHIL HAYES – THANKS FOR THE LOGO AND SUPPORT ALWAYS.

PENNY DANN – I MISS YOU TERRIBLY AND WISH I HAD MORE
CHANCES TO THANK YOU FOR YOUR BEAUTIFUL DESIGN WORK
IN THE EARLY DAYS. NEVER EVER FORGOTTEN.

AMY BELL – HOW MUCH FUN WE HAD PLAYING SHOP IN OUR FIRST STORE
AND BEYOND. GRATEFUL FROM THE BOTTOM OF MY HEART.

MEL JACKSON – THANK YOU FOR KEEPING US SANE.

...AND THANKS TO SO MANY MORE WHO WILL KNOW WHO THEY ARE.